A
Wild
Understanding

Jim Ward

Published by

Reynard & Brock Publishing

Suite A, Scarborough Business Centre
Auborough Street, Scarborough,
North Yorkshire YO11 1HT

Copyright © Jim Ward 2001

Produced by
Adverset Design & Print
Freephone 0800 0643883

ISBN1-904168-00-0

*I dedicate this book to my dear mother Winifred
whose support and love helped me to
understand God's wonderful wild creatures.*

She did not live to see me fulfil my dream.

Contents

Acknowledgements

I would like to thank

Brenda James and the people who assisted her during
the preparation of my manuscript. Without their
help my book would not have been possible.

My loyal volunteers who suffered many heartaches
over the twenty years of caring for the many wild
creatures taken into my care.

Our local coastguard, fire service and police who
helped with some of my more difficult rescues.

Jane Hairsine BVMS, MRCVS for being so tolerant
with me and my weird and wonderful wild creatures.

All branches of the media for their coverage of my
many rescues especially BBC Radio York
and The Scarborough Evening News
for their many years of loyal support.

Sir Jimmy (No 2!!) from Jim (No 1).

Last and by no means least, the Scarborough and
district residents who gave donations and gifts to
enable me to carry on my work.

Illustrations
Reproduced Courtesy of

Foreword

One of the good things about a book like this is that you never know whose hands it will fall into.

Some young person could be thinking of what to do with their life and suddenly come across this book. 'Eureka', it could happen and that would be good which is why this book will be good to lay about the world.

Sir Jimmy Savile OBE KCSG

A Wild Understanding

When interviewed on television or radio I have usually been introduced as Jim Ward, 'Wildlife Expert'. I am not an expert, but I do consider that over many years of involvement in the rescue of wild creatures I have gained an understanding, and in many cases, the hard way.

I am now in my sixty seventh year, and as I look back on my life I suppose my story begins in what was then the West Riding of Yorkshire, in a little village resting on the not-so- clean River Aire, the village of Newlay, five miles from Leeds and the same from Bradford.

I took an interest in wildlife at the age of ten and during the war years my very happy childhood was spent roaming through the local woods or playing on the river bank. I didn't realize at the time how abundant the wildlife was in those days and now, sadly, many creatures have disappeared fifty years on.

The River Aire flowed through quite a vast network of industries after leaving its tributary in Malham. I believe that the woollen industry was the main polluter. After the process of washing the wool, the waste was discharged into the river and, although the river looked like a cup of black coffee, wildlife seemed to thrive. Kingfishers were a common sight, feeding on minnows. Alongside them, herons sampled an abundance of roach and the occasional frog which might happen to pass by.

Summers seemed to be longer and certainly warmer. There was an old iron bridge across the river, built by a man called John Pollard in 1819. I can remember standing on the bridge watching hundreds of swallows catching flies; not unlike the squadrons of planes flying over at dusk carrying out their nightly raids over Germany.

I had some good childhood pals, even though they couldn't understand why I didn't join them on their bird nesting expeditions. I just could not understand why they took an egg, removed the yolk and put it in a box filled with cotton wool. I much preferred to remove an egg from a blackbird's nest and swap it for the egg of a song thrush and watch what the results were. These birds are pretty much the same in their feeding habits so no real harm was done. I was somehow christened 'the unfeathered cuckoo of Newlay'; I still don't know how to take that title.

Newlay Bridge as I remember it when I was a lad.

A Wild Understanding

As the years went by I, like many other boys, had to decide what I was going to do in the way of a job. Fortunately it was not like today when so many young people are seeking so few jobs. I decided to take an apprenticeship in Motor Engineering even though engines and gear boxes didn't come equipped with fur or feathers. I remember Mum allowing me to keep my first week's wage; I felt like the richest fifteen-year- old in the world. It didn't take me long to decide what to buy with the money: a pair of second hand binoculars, and I had some change. I still have those binoculars, which have travelled to many parts of Britain with me, and through their eyes I have seen so many wonderful creatures.

Although I was kept fully employed I still found time to study the wild creatures around me. One such creature was a water vole; for some unknown reason I christened him Boris. I struck up a real friendship with Boris in a weird sort of way. He lived on the river bank and with his constant travelling backwards and forwards had worn quite a smooth and distinctive path along the bank, so it was easy to see what his movements were.

My new found friend Boris chose to disappear on our first few encounters, but eventually he didn't mind if I sat quietly at the side of his little roadway watching him going about his business. I did however notice that he did not take kindly to any noise or movement which I made.

One day I decided to take a few biscuits to tempt Boris and to my surprise he responded by nibbling at one of the pieces laid in his roadway. After several days I gained Boris's complete trust and he would take food from my hand and even tolerate my voice when I spoke to him. Perhaps little Boris inspired me to seek that understanding of wild creatures.

Many happy years have passed by. Years in which I have had the privilege to be in direct contact with wild creatures, enabling me, because of their trust, to study and understand their ways and to see at close hand their God-given beauty.

Mum

Mum had the difficult task of bringing up two boys during the dark days of World War Two. Dad was away in the army trying to beat Hitler, while I was at home, sometimes going to school, but on the whole helping Mum with the poultry, ducks, a couple of geese, several cats and a border collie called Trixie.

Although food was rationed, something a young lad didn't really understand, we seemed to eat very well. Eggs were plentiful and the goat gave us an endless supply of milk. The very fact that we lived in a close-knit village meant everyone pulled together and shared, especially Mum, who gave some of our spare produce to those of our neighbours less fortunate than ourselves. I recollect going with her every Monday to Otley market, 'Hotton Market' to Emmerdale fans. She would always buy a few chickens for laying, or cockerels for the table and one Monday she bought a kid (a young goat). The buses in those days were rather basic with latted wooden seats. The journey from the village to Otley took about forty five minutes. It was not very comfortable! However we sat on the bus for the return journey home with the kid on Mum's knee. Conductresses were employed to take the fares because most men were in the forces. The conductress on our bus was to me a very frightening person. She had whiskers and large leather straps holding this fearsome machine which fired tickets like bullets. I thought that she could have beaten Hitler single handed. 'You'll have to pay for that dog,' she boomed. 'It's not a dog,' came the reply from my softly spoken Mum. 'A camel then,' said the conductress. Mum replied, 'It's not a camel either, it's a young goat.' The conductress muttered something which I didn't understand, and continued to bully the rest of the down-trodden passengers.

Not far from our house there was a stately home called Newlaithes Hall which was empty. Mum used to recruit me and some of my school pals for raids on the huge orchard. She was not a criminal; she just enjoyed the fun and laughs that went with these trips in the darkness. One such trip ended when the village bobby arrived; I was up a tree passing apples down to Mum at the time. Mum's excuse was that she was passing up windfallen apples for me to stick on again. The bobby appreciated her sense of humour and sent us home, but not before he had sampled a few ripe Cox's orange pippins.

Mum had a great influence on me. She helped me to understand the rights and wrongs of human behaviour towards animals. She deplored cruelty of any kind and would give a good account of herself if she saw cruelty being inflicted. She encouraged me to keep pets and showed me how to get the best from them; with kindness, understanding and, above all, patience.

As I mentioned previously, Mum was a very happy fun-loving person who loved children and readily attracted them. My friends and I would walk with her on our local river bank and she would recite funny stories which were all animal related.

Here are some examples

> I once rode a Derby winner,
> Rode it at an awful pace,
> Rode it home to get its dinner,
> Didn't ride it in the race.

> He walked into a lion's den,
> And offered it a bun,
> The lion smiled, then grew wild,
> And his day's work was done.

> He said, 'Has the dog bit you before?'
> He really was thoughtful and kind.
> He said, 'Has the dog bit you before?'
> I said, 'No sir, he's bit my behind!'

jack helping Mum (see page 24)

Mum

Towards the latter end of the war, Mum opened a small pet shop, selling fish, white mice, birdseed and accessories for dogs. She also acquired a rhesus monkey. She called him Tony because the hair on the top of his head looked as though he had a Tony Curtis style hair cut. Tony was to play a big part in Mum's life; they were inseparable. He would climb inside Mum's jumper and pounce upon anyone who got too close.

On one occasion Dad, who was on leave, got out of bed very early and brewed some tea in his pint pot. He sat down in his armchair with his pint pot of tea, and after a few minutes fell fast asleep. Tony was sitting close by; he saw his chance and as fast as lightning, grabbed the pint pot and poured the contents, tea leaves and all down the top of Dad's very baggy trousers. He retreated just as quickly up the curtains and on to the pelmet making a sound very much like childish laughter. Dad's roar could be heard for miles around.

Mum decided to diversify and sell maggots in her pet shop; catering for the local fishermen. She purchased her first consignment, put them in a very large drum with a heavy lid and then popped out for a short time. Tony decided to liberate the maggots. When Mum returned she saw hundreds of wigglers all over the floor. Tony was very unpopular that day.

In the days when Mum ran the pet shop there were very few, if any, trade warehouses, so she had to rely on trips to the larger stores in nearby Leeds. She would board the steam train at the local station, along with the bowler-hatted business men. They were all very polite to her and especially to Tony. He didn't need a ticket of course because he was under five years old, and a monkey! She would return home hours later carrying goldfish in a large tin with a pierced lid; also with several dog leads strung round her neck and pockets full of dog collars. Her profit margin must have been very small, but she was happy.

I hope that you will enjoy reading about my life with animal rescue and hope that you will also gain that, 'Wild Understanding', given to me by my Mum so long ago.

Newlay Station

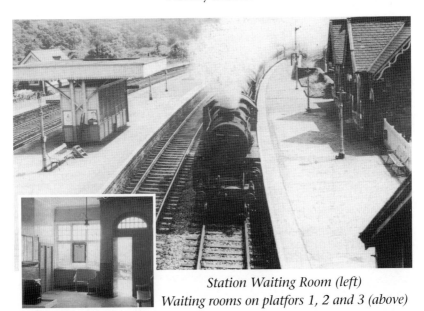

Station Waiting Room (left)
Waiting rooms on platfors 1, 2 and 3 (above)

Jim's War

During the early days of the Second World War when London was being bombed nightly many refugees were sent to the more safe regions of the country. One such family, who came from the East End of London were evacuated to our village. They were called 'The Wood Family', Mr.& Mrs. Wood and their two sons Arthur, nicknamed 'Artie,' and Mickey. Artie was ten, the same age as me, and Mickey was nine. They were allocated a cottage by our local council, so you might say they were reasonably independent.

I soon made friends with Artie although trying to understand the cockney accent proved to be quite a problem. Early on in our friendship Artie made the point that Mickey was rather slow, in fact somewhat thick. Mickey always walked in a manner resembling slow motion and was never seen without a permanent green bubble under his nose which never seemed to burst. Needless to say I always kept my distance just in case it did.

Arthur's dad, Arthur senior, was very thin and over six feet tall. He very quickly acquired the nickname, 'Big Woody'. It wasn't long before Big Woody got a job labouring at the local glue factory. He couldn't go into the army because of his flat feet.

Mrs. Wood, Cissie, was a nice person who loved to be involved with all the local children. She would take us all with her to the canal which ran parallel to the River Aire so that we could watch her dive off the bridge. We thought her very daring because the bridge appeared to be very high. One day she dived off the lower side of the bridge completely unaware that a coal barge was approaching. She was unable to see it because the wall was higher at the other side, and unable to hear the gentle put put of the engine because of the excited chatting children. Cissie reached the side and climbed out onto the bank just in time to see the barge passing by with the tubby bargee displaying his anger by shouting a number of extremely expressive words.

Like all lads we got up to all kinds of mischief; we continually sought adventure. We used to make regular sorties to the local rubbish tip where all the metal for the war effort was stored. There were old bedsteads, bikes, tin cans, etc; the list was endless. On one such visit we found an old tin bath. We agreed that it would make a fine boat and set off down to the river with Mickey trailing behind. I wasn't prepared to test our craft and neither was Artie, so we volunteered Mickey so to speak. Mickey always had the same blank expression on his face so we didn't really know if he was frightened or not. He climbed into the bath as he did every Friday night; perhaps he thought it was Friday night, we will never know. Mickey, complete with makeshift paddle and green bubble, gazed forward, never a turn of his head as he made his way downstream. I started to worry because Mickey was now out of reach. I remarked to Artie that Mickey was making for the middle of the river and approaching the weir so we both shouted to him to use the paddle. He still didn't make any attempt to guide the boat back to the river bank and when he reached the weir the boat stopped for a few seconds and then overturned, tipping Mickey into the river. Luckily the river was quite shallow. Mickey surfaced, minus bubble for once, and began to wade slowly to the river bank. Artie was very angry with Mickey. He shouted at him and accused him of losing our boat.

Mickey's Weir

Jim's War

The lads of the village formed a sort of a club, or was it a gang? We used to meet in the communal brick built air raid shelter to plan our attacks on the lads from Bramley. Bramley was a short distance from Newlay at the other side of the canal which in effect was the border of our and their territory. We never took Mickey into battle as he wasn't very good at retreating. We were also afraid that he might have given our secret plans away if he was captured; although on second thoughts there wasn't any cause for us to worry because Mickey really was in a world of his own. One of our pals, Alec Towning, was a bit like Norman Wisdom. He would come into the air raid shelter carrying a piece of chalk, draw a nail on the wall and proceed to hang his coat on the nail. This would cause the rest of the gang to howl with laughter and Alec would then sit on the floor with a puzzled expression on his face. Even Mickey could see the humour in the antics of this twelve-year-old mime artist. That air raid shelter saw more action than any other shelter in England. We held conker championships along with marble games in it when it was raining. We even had sitting quiet competitions until someone would start to giggle so the silence only lasted a few minutes. We were all experts at noise.

Looking back I don't think we understood much about the war. We all had a parent or relative in the armed forces. My step-brother was in the R.A.F. and he was stationed in England waiting to be posted to the western desert. His job was to drive a very large vehicle called a 'Queen Mary' which was designed to carry aircraft that had crashed or crash landed. These aircraft were used for spares because parts were very scarce in the early days of the war.

I remember one special day; the headmaster sent for me and I thought, 'What have I done now?' My knees began to knock as I made my way to the headmaster's office because he used the cane to punish us very often. The headmaster, Mr. Walker who was nicknamed Pip, thundered, 'Come in,' when I knocked on his office door. I very nervously opened the door and went in. There to my surprise standing next to Pip was my step-brother. I discovered that he was returning to an airfield near Lincoln with his vehicle which was loaded with the remains of a Fairey Battle Bomber. Pip allowed everyone in the school to look round this super aircraft. I was the proudest lad in England that day and the most popular.

Newlaithes Hall was in a state of neglect and disrepair. It was eventually taken over by the military, and I suppose, in a way it was a good thing because the soldiers tidied up the vast gardens. They also erected huts for living accommodation and The Hall was used for officers and administration.

The gang spent quite a lot of time at The Hall. We made friends with many of the soldiers and collected souvenirs from them in the form of badges and buttons which represented the regiments which were passing through on their way to various battle fronts. We were amazed at some of the big guns that were at the camp with some of the artillery regiments. One regiment had its own bugler who played reveille early in the morning and followed on with some of the popular tunes which were played on the wartime radio. He proved to be very popular with the villagers.

Not long after the last regiment left high barbed wire fences were erected around the camp and the village's first prisoners of war started to arrive. Artie and I used to stand near the gates to watch them arrive. We had heard the stories on the news about the bad things the Germans were doing but through a young lad's eyes these men with sad, pale faces didn't look any different to my Dad or my step brother, Dennis. After a few weeks and many visits to the camp I would stand near the fence and watch the activity going on inside. The gardens were once more returning to their former glory.

It was on one such visit that I met Eddie. He was a prisoner and in my eyes, a giant. He approached the fence and in a very soft, deep voice said, 'Hello, I am Eddie.' I did not reply for several seconds as I thought he might want me to help him escape. Eventually I replied and gave him my name. For several minutes we tried to make conversation; Eddie knew a little English but I knew not a word of German except, 'Heil Hitler', which I didn't think Eddie would appreciate, so I kept that to myself. I met Eddie as often as I could; sometimes I took Artie with me but he didn't seem impressed. Perhaps he still had memories of the London Blitz, something I didn't understand and which was never discussed.

As my friendship with Eddie strengthened I managed to find a small hole in the fence. I used this to sneak into the camp under the cover of darkness. Eddie was the camp's barber so he gave me quite a few free hair cuts. I also gathered together many German badges and buttons, much to the envy of my pals. Sometimes while I was having my hair cut we would hear the guard approaching so Eddie would put me in the corner of the room and cover me with a large overcoat. I'm sure the guards knew I was there but a lad of my tender years couldn't organize a mass escape and I'm quite sure that these prisoners didn't want to escape anyway.

The months seemed to pass so quickly and Christmas was very near. To the surprise of everyone in the village the local council announced that the military were going to allow the German prisoners into our homes if they were invited. Mum invited my friend Eddie and his room-mate Godfreid who was only sixteen. In the weeks before Christmas the prisoners were very busy making and painting toys. They scrounged whatever materials they could, from biscuit tins to old pieces of wood. The finished products were really beautiful. On Christmas Day the prisoners distributed the toys to the children in the village and surrounding areas.

Dad was on leave and when Eddie and Godfreid arrived for dinner on Christmas Day it was quite a sight to see two German soldiers in uniform sitting at the same table as a British soldier. What a strange combination. After we had eaten a truly wonderful meal Dad made a sort of speech. He wished our two guests a Happy Christmas and tried to make them understand that he wished they could be with their own families. This was too much for young Godfreid who became very emotional. He was comforted by Mum and the day went really well.

Not many weeks after Christmas I went to the camp and was very surprised to find it deserted. The prisoners had moved out just as quickly as they came. This was very upsetting for me because I had not been able to say goodbye to Eddie and there was no way of contacting him. I have often wondered about Eddie; I hope that he was able to return to his own family.

As I mentioned earlier my headmaster, Pip Walker, was quite a tyrant. He certainly was very liberal with the cane which he called his Two Pennorth, which when translated means two pennies worth in old money. I certainly had shares in his cane. Big Woody was a keen gardener and gave a lot of his produce to the locals and to Artie's teacher, Miss Lineham. One morning after assembly Pip called in what he called his waifs and strays. This was his sarcastic way of calling in the children who hadn't quite made it into assembly. On this occasion Artie was among the waifs and strays and he was marched in front of Pip who had his Two Pennorth at the ready. Artie was carrying a large brown paper bag. Pip roared, 'Now then, Wee Willy Wood, what have you got in your brown paper bag?' As he spoke Pip prodded Artie's bag with his Two Pennorth causing it to burst open and its contents which were gooseberries spilled out onto the floor and rolled everywhere. Artie still holding the very empty bag replied, 'Goosegogs sir.' He was caned for bearing gifts.

With the departure of the German prisoners life seemed pretty dull. We got bored battling with the Bramley lads and an unconditional truce developed. The grown-ups continually worked for the war effort. They press ganged me and my pals into collecting jam jars; they said this would help to raise the money needed to buy a Corvette for the navy. This puzzled me because when I took my jam jars to the rag man the best he could do was to give me a balloon or a pint pot.

One day during school playtime I saw what I thought was a tug of war and the two participants were putting a great deal of effort into it. They weren't pulling a rope but something which looked like a long, coloured piece of string about fifteen yards in length. There was quite a crowd of children watching so I thought I would liven up the proceedings. I took out my trusty penknife and cut the string which made the two lads fall on their bottoms amid loud laughter and applause. I was laughing the loudest until I noticed that the string wasn't string but a very stretched scarf.

Once more I got caned by Pip Walker and my poor Mum had to pay for another scarf. That taught me that I should not have gone in head first. I have of course gone in head first many times during my life. So does one ever learn by one's mistakes?

On reflection; people have often said to me, 'Would you like to turn the clock back.' My answer is always the same, 'Yes I would; with no regrets.'

Jack

I believe that every naturalist or conservationist will have committed some sort of selfish or neglectful act during their lifetime. I, for one, must admit to an early misdemeanour.

As a boy of twelve, I had always wanted a pet wild bird and I listened to stories about lads taking and taming magpies and jackdaws. Today, when all birds are protected by the Wildlife and Countryside Act 1981, it is an offence to take eggs or young birds from their nests. No such law existed in the days of my childhood, so really I feel I may be excused for removing a very young jackdaw from its nest.

It was mid May when I made the short journey from our village to a local abbey called Kirkstall Abbey. This beautiful building has a very high main tower, with a lightning conductor. I sat on a wall for several minutes watching the jackdaws flying in and out of their nests. I noted that there was a nest very close to the lightning conductor, so I began to climb.

By the time I was half way to my goal my arms ached but I felt I must carry on. I finally reached the nest which contained two very young birds. Their eyes were barely open and there was certainly a shortage of feathers. I lifted one bird from the nest, tucked it inside my shirt and started to make my descent. I found this quite difficult because I was continually being attacked by several jackdaws and at one stage nearly lost my grip.

When I arrived home and told Mum that I had taken a young jackdaw from its nest she was very angry and told me to put it back immediately. She had second thoughts when I explained to her where I had climbed to get it. Mum really made me feel guilty and I was made to realize that I had been very foolish and irresponsible. She did however give me so much support in the weeks that followed. She taught me how to mix Jack's food, which consisted of a rather mushy mix of boiled potatoes, hard boiled eggs and a little bran. My new baby had to be hand fed every hour during the hours of daylight. Mum fed him while I was at school and I would take over after school and at weekends. Within a period of about three weeks Jack became fully feathered and was able to feed himself which was quite a bonus to us, his weary foster parents.

Jack

It wasn't long before Jack was making short but clumsy flights in the garden. The house soon became out of bounds because some of Mum's treasures were in danger of disappearing.

August saw my school holidays, so I was able to give all my time to Jack. He would perch on my shoulder as I rode my bike around the village or into the local woods. Jack became very popular with everyone and he would greet them with a very loud 'Jack!'

At the end of the day he made his way to my pigeon cote which was a very large wooden barrel on a tall post. The pigeons weren't very friendly towards Jack but they tolerated him. He would fly to the barrel and evict several before settling down for the night. In the morning at sunrise he would evict all the pigeons before flying to my bedroom and demanding food.

During those long hot summer days a local ice-cream man came to the village. His mode of transport was a van and he rang a bell to let everyone know he had arrived. Jack would wait for him perched on the roof of a large Victorian house overlooking the valley.

When Jack heard the bell he flew down to the van and the ice-cream man gave him an empty cone. Jack took the cone by the open end and flew off with the pointed end facing forward, this made him look like a black woodpecker as he made his way back to his lofty perch.

Jack's popularity came to an end one Monday morning, washing day. Jack had never shown any interest in the lines of washing hanging outside the row of ten houses opposite our house, until this particular Monday morning. For some reason only known to himself Jack started pulling out clothes pegs at one end of the row and didn't stop until he was at the other end, where he became trapped in a lady's very precious nylon stocking. He had been caught in the act. It wasn't long before a deputation of very irate ladies came knocking on our door seeking revenge. Jack by this time had retreated to the pigeon cote and I to my bedroom. I waited for some time before Mum summoned me for a talk. As ever, Mum came up with a solution. Jack was to be kept in on Mondays, although some of the ladies made other suggestions as to his fate. Mum's solution worked well and everybody was quite satisfied.

Things soon got back to normal, or as normal as it could be living with a spoilt jackdaw.

I decided one day to paint my bike. Pale blue was the chosen colour, or was it the only paint I had at the time? Like many other commodities, paint was very scarce during the war. I had almost finished when there was a loud cry from Jack and at the same time an even louder cry from Mum. I looked to see what was happening. Jack had stood in the tin of paint, flown through the open front door and landed on the piano, much to the horror of my Mum. He then flew out again, retreating to the large Victorian house. When Mum had calmed down and I had come out of hiding, she laughed and said, 'You now have a jackdaw with blue gloss legs, something of a rarity, I think.' Jack stayed out of everyone's way for about three days.

It wasn't long before the next crisis arose. The local odd job man discovered an assortment of cuff links, ear-rings, tea spoons and various other curious objects whilst he was cleaning out our gutters. He showed these objects to Mum who immediately exclaimed, 'Jack!' My next task was to put all these objects in a cardboard box and go to every house in the village, asking the occupants if any of the objects in the box belonged to them. The box soon emptied and I had to endure some very rude remarks from the reunited owners.

One day Jack failed to return to the pigeon cote which was not unusual but after several days I began to get extremely upset. Mum decided to put an advert in the local press under 'Lost and found'. In those days there were no radio help lines. Two days after the advert went into the paper, Mum received a card from the RSPCA in Leeds, asking her to call in as they had a jackdaw which was very tame. She gave me my tram fare and I set off with my heart in my mouth. I arrived at the RSPCA and was met by a very large man in a blue sweater and a pimple on his nose. In a deep voice he asked me what I had come for. 'A jackdaw,' I said. 'What sort of jackdaw?' he said. 'One with blue legs,' I replied. This brought a roar of laughter from the large man. He disappeared into a back room and reappeared with a cardboard box with holes in the top. I peered in and there was Jack, complete with blue enamel legs.

Jack

Many months went by. Jack and I had many adventures together until Jack failed to return to the pigeon cote, this time without trace. Mum consoled a very upset son, by telling him that Jack may well have found a mate.

Unknown to Mum I made many trips to Kirkstall Abbey, looking for a jackdaw, with blue enamel legs.

Jack's Viewing Platform

Aire of the Dog

I was just twelve years old when I carried out my first rescue. It was late evening; my two pals and I were sitting on a low wall near the bridge. The weir is about two hundred yards down the river from the bridge and as the river was in flood the water flowing over the weir sounded like an express train.

As we sat and talked we thought we could hear barking and whimpering. We didn't take any notice of it at first but the cries persisted so we decided to investigate. The cries led us down the the path alongside the river. We stopped at a point below the weir where there were some very overgrown willow trees, their branches trailing in the swollen river.

It had become quite dark so one of my pals ran home and returned with a torch and shone it in the direction of the barking. To our amazement we saw a puppy caught up among some driftwood. Without hesitation I grabbed hold of some of the upper branches and edged my way along one of the thicker lower branches. I was about three feet above the water and as I made my way along the branch it began to bend.

Willow is very supple and can stand a lot of weight before breaking. Perhaps if it had been any other tree I might not have been so lucky.

By the time I had reached the puppy my feet were touching the water and they were very cold. I grabbed the poor, wet creature which was too weak to struggle and put it in my jumper. The journey back to the river bank took much longer as I had to hold the bottom of my jumper to prevent the puppy from falling out.

My pals and I ran to my house and excitedly told Mum the story. The look on her face told me that she was angry but relieved that her silly but brave young son hadn't fallen in the river. She thanked my two pals and sent them home before drying out the very soggy, very cold twosome.

Mum gave me a hot cup of milk and sent me to bed with the assurance that things would be sorted out in the morning. I awoke very early and raced downstairs to find my new friend. Mum had put him in the shoe cupboard next to the fireplace with some old shirts for a bed. I was greeted with a very wet lick.

When Mum came into the room my first question was, 'Can we keep him?'

She very gently answered, 'He may already belong to someone and might have to be returned to his owner.'

No one claimed the puppy. Sadly I wasn't allowed to keep him, but there was a happy ending. A very loving home was found for the water baby of the River Aire.

Puppy rescue took place on the right further downstream.

Riverside to Seaside

I, like many other young men of my age group, had no other option but to do two years National Service, as it was compulsory. I decided to sign on as a regular soldier for three years. I was fortunate and proud to serve in The Royal Artillery and for a short period on attachment to The King's Troop Royal Horse Artillery, which I thoroughly enjoyed.

On leaving HM forces I went to work as a lorry driver with a steel company; although I was a qualified diesel engineer I could earn more money driving lorries. I stayed with the company for twenty years, finally becoming their Executive Sales Director. Unfortunately steel became nationalized and Idecided I no longer wanted to be a part of the rat race. I was in desperate need of a complete change and I felt I was being drawn back to Sewerby because of my fond childhood memories.

Sewerby is a village on the coast in the East Riding of Yorkshire. It attracts many visitors who come to visit Sewerby Hall and Park. Flamborough is a larger village which is found a few miles along the coast; it is steeped in a fishing tradition going back many generations. It has a delightful cove with brilliant white pebbles and a magical cave with two entries, one facing out to sea and the other facing the sand.

Mum's two sisters lived at Sewerby and we had many enjoyable holidays there. During the war I was lucky to be able to go there for a week's holiday on my own and stay with my eccentric Aunt Amelia, locally known as the 'Duchess', whom I loved very dearly. Mum used to put me on the bus in Leeds and my Aunt Amelia used to be waiting for me at the other end. Like Mum she kept a few chickens and ducks. She ran a thriving village shop with my Uncle Edgar who used to be on the stage. He was an illusionist and the piece de resistance of his act was 'The Cage Of Death'. The shop sold everything from a newspaper to a leg of pork.

Aunt Amelia loved going to the sale rooms and bought all manner of things including an enormous stuffed eagle with outstretched wings. She gave it to me to take home and I struggled up the steps of the bus because I thought there would be more room on the double back seat on the top deck for us. I was subjected to some surprised and confused stares by my fellow passengers. At the end of journey I stepped off the bus in Leeds to be greeted by Mum. Her comment about the eagle was, 'That's typical of my sister.' I politely asked her if I could keep the eagle. I knew she wouldn't make me take it back.

———

We have all heard the saying 'We all make mistakes'. I for one made a fatal mistake when I had been living in Flamborough for only a few weeks. I loved to walk on the beach, it seemed so pure and uncomplicated. So right! It all came to an abrupt end one day when I spotted what looked like a small penguin. The poor creature was covered in thick oil which had a consistency similar to tar.

I took the bird home and consulted my bird book and discovered that my penguin was in fact a guillemot, one of Britain's most common diving birds. I removed the oil with warm soapy water, and then rinsed it with the aid of a shower head. The end result was quite astounding. The bird was now a smart black and white instead of the dirty, oily creature I had recently rescued.

After allowing it to dry in front of the coal fire I proudly returned to the beach and released it back into the sea. The bird swam for about fifty yards and then to my horror it began to struggle and became waterlogged and drowned before my very eyes. There wasn't anything I could do other than walk away. I was devastated after witnessing the death of a creature I had rescued only two hours before.

I immediately started to research into the cleaning and care of oil polluted birds, and discovered that by washing my bird I had removed its natural oil.

Through experience I learned that, depending on the quantity of oil causing the damage, and the level of stress suffered by the bird, it can be anything from twenty four hours to several months before the preen gland once again begins secreting the natural oil. This gland is located on the bird's rump, and when the bird preens itself it takes in its beak a globule of oil from the gland and spreads it along its feathers, repeating this process several times until all the feathers are coated. A bird is not waterproof without its natural oil.

Yes, I made a tragic mistake but I made sure it was never repeated! This tragedy affected me so profoundly that I decided to dedicate my life to the rescue and care of wild creatures.

I decided to moved fifteen miles up the coast to live on the outskirts of Scarborough because I was offered a job that included living accommodation; this was a large Victorian house with about two and a half acres of land, part of which provided a home for my rescued animals and the rest for growing vegetables.

Scarborough is a well-loved holiday resort situated on the North Yorkshire coast. It is a historic town, known to the Romans, and has developed through invasion, civil war and rebellion, with great expansion in Victorian/Edwardian times, to the present day.

I knew, having established myself in Scarborough, that I was prepared and able to meet whatever challenges I would certainly encounter in the future.

A Timeless Tale

I always made a point of not giving pet names to rescued wild animals until I was certain that they were going to survive. Not that I felt it was a waste of time, but if a creature died and it had a name it was just a little harder for me to accept.

Two very young fox cubs, a vixen and a dog, were brought into my animal charity shop after a violent rain storm one day in May. They arrived at different times and were brought in by two different members of the public. It transpired that they had been found in the same area and I could only assume that they were members of the same family. Perhaps they had been washed out of their home by a flash flood?

I immediately dried the babies under a heat lamp and then bottle-fed them with goat's milk. It wasn't long before I was able to feed them with fresh minced chicken. Foxes, like many other wild animals, develop and mature very quickly. I decided it was time for name choosing and there were quite a few suggestions from friends. Some were original, some were not and some were quite ridiculous. As I mentioned earlier I thought they were from the same family and, because they were brought to me at different times, I christened them Tick and Tock.

How's that for being un-original?

Tick and Tock were like all youngsters, boisterous and mischievous. Max, my Alsatian, was five years old, above average size and a gentle giant. He wasn't very athletic but more of a dog that liked to lie and watch the world go by. Tick and Tock had other ideas for Max and when the three of them were in the kitchen they would take it in turns to try and pull him by his tail around the vinyl floor. Max would sometimes lie with either Tick or Tock in his huge mouth, treating them like lollipops until they were soggy at the front, dry at the rear.

Time went by very quickly and I knew that the time had arrived for me to start thinking about a release date for Tick and Tock. It would have been so easy for me to keep them but I knew that was selfishness on my part. I have said so many times to so many people that wild animals must live in the wild. There are plenty of dogs and cats desperately in need of a loving home.

I visited several sites where I thought Tick and Tock could be released. The site I eventually chose was an area of seventy five acres which contained a number of disused gravel pits, heavy scrub and large boulders. Also there was an abundance of rabbits which meant that Tick and Tock would not have to go scavenging in urban areas.

I chose an autumn evening to release Tick and Tock and made sure that they were not over fed to encourage them to find food for themselves. With my heart in my boots but thinking that this is the bonus of a job well done I released my adopted Tick and Tock. At first they seemed reluctant to go but that sense of freedom prevailed and they both disappeared into the thick gorse bushes. I did not hang about and left with a heavy heart.

Many months passed by and on one late spring evening I was driving home and approaching a roundabout. This was some short distance from the gravel pits where I had released my two cubs. I saw two foxes sitting on the roundabout and I stopped the car and got out. Were these two foxes Tick and Tock? I couldn't resist calling out their names, 'Tick,Tock. Tick,Tock. Tick, Tock.' They looked and hesitated for a few seconds before they ran through a nearby hedge and into the darkness beyond. I carried on my way convinced that I had seen Tick and Tock because totally wild foxes would have run away immediately.

Some days later I was approached by my friend, the village bobby. He had a very concerned look on his face and asked me if I was all right. I assured him that I was and asked him why he was so concerned about me. His reply was that he had spoken to two colleagues who were on motor patrol. They had been parked near the roundabout that same evening and had seen me stop my car, get out and then heard me shout, 'Tick,Tock' several times, but they had not seen the foxes. This led them to put a question to my constable friend, 'Does Jim Ward think he's a clock?'

Is this a timeless tale or just priceless?

Max with Tick or is it Tock?

Swan on the Derwent

In April 1985 we were having some very heavy showers and on the fourteenth I received a phone call from the local police. There was a swan in difficulties on the River Derwent, close to the village of West Heslerton.

I wasn't prepared for what I saw on arrival at the site. The river was in flood, almost at the point of bursting its banks. The swan was in the middle of the river, entangled in a small bush, with what appeared to be a broken wing. There was nothing I could do alone, so I returned to base and made a couple of phone calls to two chaps who I could always count on to help; what they lacked in their knowledge of rescues they made up in enthusiasm.

This rescue would give me the chance to christen a new inflatable dinghy which had recently been donated. So equipped with dinghy, ropes and enthusiasm, we set off to rescue our swan.

When we arrived our swan was looking very sorry for himself. The river was flowing very fast so a direct approach with the dinghy was impossible. Several suggestions were made by my volunteers, including, 'Let's lasso it!' Reply, 'What from fifty yards? I'm not Roy Rogers!'

We finally agreed on the best course of action, and took the dinghy downstream, along the river bank to a bridge. We fastened two ropes to the front of the dinghy so that it could be pulled upstream by two people, one on either side of the river bank. The third person would sit in the dinghy. Who was it to be in the dinghy? Yes, you've guessed. ME!

I climbed into the dinghy, knelt down and off we went. Everything was going to plan, with my volunteers slowly making their way upstream. I was about fifteen to twenty feet away from the swan when it began to panic. Suddenly it became free and made a desperate attempt to swim away from its rescuer. When my two volunteers saw what was happening their enthusiasm went into top gear. They started to run faster and faster until the dinghy, not designed as a ski boat, started to nose dive with me kneeling in the bows. Down I went, up I came spitting out bits of driftwood and rubbish from the flooded river. As I surfaced for what I thought was the last time I realized that the swan was alongside the dinghy.

As I made a desperate attempt to grab him, the dinghy capsized. I managed to hold onto the struggling bird with one arm and the dinghy with the other and shouted to my trusty high speed volunteers to pull me ashore.

To say the least, the rescue was a little traumatic for both myself and the swan. Sadly his wing had been damaged beyond repair but after receiving treatment from my vet we were very lucky to be able to release him on a large private lake in the grounds of a local stately home. There he would live out his remaining years in peace

A Bushy Tailed Houdini

This story is about a very special fox called Dalby. I called him Dalby because my story begins in Dalby Forest. It was around midsummer when I received a call from one of the forest rangers. He told me that a very large fox was scrounging from one of the picnic areas in the forest. I thought, 'Was it a fox or was it Yogi Bear?'

As I drove to the forest ranger's cottage I couldn't help thinking, 'Why was a fox taking risks begging food from the very creatures who wear red jackets, toot horns and allow their hounds to rampage across the countryside in pursuit of him and his family? Perhaps this wasn't a fox but a small, lost Alsatian. No, I shouldn't doubt the ranger.'

When I arrived at the ranger's cottage a six foot gentleman with a smiling face and a swarthy complexion came out to greet me. We shook hands, went inside and drank tea while the ranger told me about the fox. Not only did he take food from the picnickers hands, he also climbed into cars if the doors were open; campers were his speciality. After about half an hour the ranger looked at his watch and said,'It's 4.30pm, he should be due about now.' My mouth dropped in amazement. 'What do you mean, due about now?' 'Oh yes, he usually arrives at the picnic area at about 11.30am and 4.30pm.'

It took us about ten minutes to walk to the picnic area. A couple of elderly people were eating sandwiches at a table and the ranger greeted them with a smile and asked if they had seen a fox? They looked at him rather bemused and replied, 'Not today.' I think they must have thought they were on Candid Camera. We chatted for a while and suddenly the ranger said, 'Here he comes.' He pointed to a narrow path which led to a small lake and sure enough here came Dalby, the largest, the most beautiful fox I had ever seen. Dalby didn't hesitate. He walked straight up to the elderly lady who was, I think, eating a cucumber sandwich. She said to the ranger, 'What shall I do?' He said, 'Offer him some food, he won't bite you.' Dalby gently took the bread from the lady and waited for more. Twenty minutes later Dalby decided to leave and went back along the same path. The silence lasted several minutes before the ranger said, 'Well, what do you think?' I really didn't know what to think. The ranger was very concerned for Dalby's welfare. He knew that even though hunting never reached that part of the forest there were characters who would not hesitate to harm him.

We returned to the ranger's cottage to discuss the situation over another cup of tea. I always believe tea is a great solver of problems and after several suggestions from me we finally agreed that I would come the next day and take Dalby into my care until a suitable safe haven could be found. The following morning I went back to the cottage and went with the ranger to the picnic area. We took with us a large cage in which to transport Dalby and placed it several yards away. We didn't have long to wait. Dalby arrived at almost 11.15am. This was uncanny. I produced a large piece of chicken which Dalby ate. I then walked towards the cage, throwing pieces of chicken as I went, Dalby followed. Dalby ate the last piece and then looked at the cage for a few seconds. It was quite weird. It seemed as if he was trying to work out what this object was, or had he seen something like it before? He about turned and walked back along his path and disappeared.

I told the ranger that I would work out another plan and return in time for Dalby's next visit at 4.30pm. I went home and rang my friendly vet. I explained the situation and asked him if he could give me some sort of tranquillizer which would make it easier and possibly less traumatic for Dalby. The vet gave me one tablet and said that it was very strong and would be sufficient. When I arrived I saw the ranger waiting for me with Dalby sitting close to him. I explained to the ranger what my intentions were. I placed the tablet inside a tender piece of chicken and gave it to Dalby, and waited. He hung around for several minutes before making his way back along the path. The ranger said, 'Oh dear, it's not going to work.' I was about to agree when Dalby started to stagger. I slowly followed him for about fifty yards until he stopped, lay down and literally went to sleep.

It didn't take long for us to take Dalby back to the car and lay him full length on the back seat. It was getting dusk and the ranger invited me to partake in the ritual cup of tea or two before I returned home. After about an hour I decided to make a move. It was very dark by this time and the ranger said he would get a torch. He opened the door and to our surprise we saw a fox sitting on the door step. 'Oh no!' I said, 'Not another one.' The fox calmly walked past us and lay down in front of the fire. We both stood in silence for several seconds. I looked at the ranger and said, 'Dalby?' We went to the car and sure enough the rear door was open. In the weeks to come little did I know what a merry dance Dalby was going to lead me.

I drove home with Dalby and introduced him to the living quarters I had prepared for him. It was in the rear yard of the house. The yard was surrounded by a ten foot wall so it was quite an easy task to put wire netting across the top, also there was a small outbuilding which was an ideal place for my new guest to sleep. The back door of the house led directly into the yard so when I was at home Dalby had free access to the house.

We got on quite well together. In the evenings I would sit and write notes about my work and Dalby would doze in front of the fire. Sometimes I couldn't help noticing that Dalby would be sitting staring directly at me and when I caught his stare he would slowly blink his eyes and settle down. If only I knew what this poor wild creature was thinking; was he troubled, was he sad? I would never know. One morning my friendly vet made a social call and I couldn't wait to show off Dalby to him. When he saw Dalby he was quite impressed. I mention to him that I thought Dalby was very different and said that foxes were usually very hyperactive, but not my Dalby. After handling Dalby for a few minutes the vet asked, 'Did you know this chap has been neutered?' This diagnosis immediately answered my question as to why Dalby was so tame. He had been taken as a cub and hand reared. A practice I strongly disagree with. Dogs and cats are for pets, not foxes.

The big question now was, why was a neutered fox living in Dalby forest? Had he been purposely abandoned, or was he just lost? The following day I contacted our local B.B.C. radio station and newspaper office and told them the story of Dalby in the hope that his owners would come and claim him but there was no response. However, I did received many offers of adoption. The weeks went by very quickly. I was preparing breakfast one snowy morning just before Christmas and Dalby was dozing in front of the fire as usual, or so I thought. I finished my breakfast and shouted for Dalby. I waited for a few minutes and then decided to go and look for him. I searched every room of the house, eight altogether; there wasn't a sign of Dalby. As I mentioned earlier the house was Victorian and it still had all its original features including the fireplaces in each of the four bedrooms. It was then that my first fear struck me. Had Dalby gone up the chimney? I knelt in the fireplace and listened. Not a sound. I shouted his name. Not a sound. I then went into the loft with a hammer and chisel and removed several bricks from the internal labyrinth of the chimney breasts. No Dalby. I went outside, looked up and saw pawprints in the snow, they started on the roof and went downwards onto the outbuilding and along the road. Dalby was free again but for what fate?

I searched the surrounding countryside for several hours, I did not catch a glimpse of Dalby. As I was making my way home I met a local chap who spent most of his life in the pub or off- licence. He greeted me with, 'Good morning, Mr Ward.' I returned the greeting. He then said, 'I saw a very strange thing earlier this morning.' 'Oh what was that?' I replied. 'A fox came out of your chimney and ran up the road.' I asked, 'Was it carrying a sack on its back?' The man walked off scratching his head. I arrived home feeling very tired and then it hit me, a sudden lonely empty feeling came over me. Did I take Dalby for granted? Was that why he gave me those questioning stares? My negative thoughts were brought to an abrupt end when the telephone started to ring. It was a lady from the local village of Cayton who was a member of the local field naturalists. She had rung to say that she was looking out of her kitchen window and saw a jet black fox leaving black pawprints in the snow. Once again I contacted the local media and told them of Dalby's escape. A short time after the local radio station broadcast details of Dalby my phone never stopped ringing. Calls came from as far away as Malton.

One irate lady accused Dalby of killing her cat and another one said that her dustbin had been upturned. The two callers lived about fifteen miles apart. In fact, I was waiting for the someone to accuse him of being responsible for the great train robbery. Finally one caller told me that Dalby at that moment was sitting on the roof of her outhouse. I took her address and set off to collect my bushy tailed worry maker. The house was almost in the centre of Scarborough, and I arrived only to find that he had disappeared again. I thanked the lady and returned home a very disappointed man.

It was about two days later when I received a phone call from the whipper-in at the local hunt kennels. He said in a very calm voice, 'Will you come and collect your fox. The Master will be very angry if he sees him here.' I nervously said, "Where?" He said, 'At my house, he's in front of my fire.' I was almost in a state of shock. The hunt kennels would certainly be the last place I would go if I were a fox, but I was not Dalby. I arrived at the kennels and sure enough there was Dalby fast asleep in front of the log fire. I apologised to the whipper-in. He said he would appreciate it if I kept this to myself because not only would he be in trouble with the hunt committee he also felt he wouldn't be able to face his pals in the pub. I assured him that the secret was safe with me as I was only too happy to be reunited with Dalby. The next few weeks passed without incident.

I moved house to start a wildlife sanctuary which was by coincidence close to the place in the forest were I first met Dalby. The place was quite run-down; it consisted of an acre of land and a small cottage. I built Dalby a very large compound to himself with various items of furniture: some very large logs for him to climb or just to lounge on and two large concrete pipes for him to use as a type of bolt hole. Not that he really needed to bolt as he was never in any danger. His sleeping accommodation was a substantial stone structure packed with bales of straw for warmth. He was never short of company as there was always the occasional badger or fox cub recuperating after having veterinary treatment for various injuries or illnesses. Dalby was extremely kind to them all. It was as if he knew of their plight; he was their kind.

Everything seemed to be going quite well until one morning I went to feed Dalby only to find that the compound door was open. Dalby had once more decided to leave home and he had somehow managed to slide the bolt on the door. The only consolation for me was that he had plenty of forest to roam in, and, of course, he was always welcome if he decided to return. This was too simple for Dalby because within twenty four hours he once more appeared at the hunt kennels. A very embarrassed me collected him and I was given a stern warning; the hunt would not be held responsible for Dalby's safety. By this time I was feeling very sad for the poor mixed up creature; some unknown person had interfered with him and left him for someone else to worry about. What was I to do? Should I take him to my vet and have him put to sleep for his own safety? Even though I cared so much for him it seemed that his quality of life was almost nil. I did not sleep that night and the morning arrived all too quickly. I went to Dalby's compound and sat on one of his logs. It didn't take Dalby long to join me and with a sniff to reassure himself it was me he sat at my feet and looked into the misty forest. He then turned and looked at me exactly the same way as he did several months before. I patted him as a person pats their faithful Labrador and shed a tear or two. I had finally made my decision, 'Dalby, old pal, we will see this through.'

I made his compound more secure and what spare time I had I spent it with Dalby. We played silly games together which he enjoyed and I hoped that he might have forgotten his urge to wander. Several weeks passed and Dalby seemed much more settled. One very misty morning I was called out to a very badly injured seal pup near Filey. By the time I had rescued the seal and taken it to the vet it was late afternoon. The poor seal subsequently died of its injuries. I returned to the sanctuary and found Dalby's compound door open. This was no natural escape as the padlock had been deliberately broken. This time I feared the worst. Had someone taken him or had they simply released him? I knew that if he had been released he would certainly be identified by members of the local community because he was wearing a collar with a disc which had the animal sanctuary details on it.

Several days went by and then weeks. Not a word or a sign of my dear mixed up Dalby. Several years on I can still see that searching look in his eyes. I still visit the forest and walk the paths we walked together so many times. I can somehow feel his presence, which will, I hope, stay forever. I still miss my bushy tailed Houdini.

My First Seal

I have over the years rescued many seals both large and small. However there is always a first time.....

I was called out to the rocks at Ravenscar, one of the most inaccessible parts of the North Yorkshire coast, where a young seal was in some difficulties. The seal was about three months old and old enough to give a good account of itself. Incidentally the seal was a Farne Islands grey and they are not as friendly as a common seal. In fact it has been said that the common seal should be called the 'friendly seal'.

I approached with caution and when I was only a few feet from my patient he or she started to growl like a Rottweiler with a bone. That was when the adrenalin started to flow, but outwardly I felt I had to look the part and appear calm and professional because a few people were starting to take an interest in the rescue. My rescue equipment at that time consisted of a net, a rope and a pair of gardening gloves. After a few falls and many submissions I managed to get the seal into the net. I then started the long climb back to the rescue vehicle, made my patient comfortable and drove the eleven miles to my sanctuary.

In wildlife and animal rescue it is always the practice to put the individual into quiet isolation before giving treatment or food. When it is decided that the patient is settled enough, treatment can commence and, of course, feeding. In many cases force feeding is necessary and it is certainly the case with all seals.

When I felt that it was time to start feeding my seal I turned to an expert for advice, the curator of what was then Flamingo Park Zoo, now called Flamingoland. He said that the seal would have to be force-fed and warned me that this was a difficult operation needing two people, a bucket of sprats and two pieces of strong towel. One person has to sit astride the seal with a piece of towel in their hands and when the seal opens its mouth to bite they very quickly put the towel around the bottom jaw until the seal's teeth pierce the towel, then holding the towel securely with one hand, place the other piece of towel around the upper jaw. You now have control of opening and closing the seal's mouth and the other person can insert the fish.

The trouble was that my concentration was solely on the feeding and not on staying on the seal's back. He or she bucked like a rodeo pony and eventually threw me over its back into a muddy puddle. It then proceeded to chase me around the sanctuary. Never let it be said that seals are slow on land. Flamingo Park Zoo kindly provided a home for my seal until it was strong enough to be released.

Since that escapade I have gained much knowledge in the rescue of seals but, as I mentioned earlier, there is always a first time.

grey seal

common seal

Gulliver

One of the most interesting aspects of wildlife rescue is the variety of challenges. When the phone rings it could be a call to rescue a fox, a deer or a seal in distress. The list is endless. There is always something that needs rescuing, twenty four hours a day, seven days a week. Our busiest times were in May and June. This is when the nesting season is in full swing and young birds get themselves into all sorts of trouble, sometimes through no fault of their own.

This brings me to the story of one such herring gull, Gulliver. At the time of this particular incident I had somewhere in the region of thirty young herring gulls. They had either been abandoned or fallen from roof-top nests in the centre of Scarborough. However, one very sunny morning I was feeling quite pleased, because in spite of being very busy, things seemed to be running quite smoothly. That was until I was confronted by a very irate gentleman. His first words were, 'Are you the animal man?' 'Yes, I am the animal man,' I replied. My imagination ran riot. I pictured myself with a hairy body and paws chasing cats up trees. The next statement from the man was, 'I have a roof repair business and my men are threatening to strike!. 'Why?' I asked. 'It's them gulls!' he replied. 'What gulls?' I asked. He explained that his men refused to do any repairs to the roof of one of Scarborough's tallest buildings because a pair of herring gulls were attacking them.

I explained that the birds were most certainly rearing young. I assured him that they would not attack his men physically, and were only trying to drive them away. He asked me to go with him to the site to explain this to his men. I agreed. When we arrived we were met by three very large men. Any one of them appeared capable of wrestling an alligator. I gave them exactly the same explanation, but they were determined not to work until the birds had been removed. The boss spoke, 'What are you going to do?' I suggested that he should leave the work for a few weeks until the nest was empty, but unfortunately this was not possible. The four of them went into quiet conference, and eventually the boss said, 'I will get the council to get rid of them!' I knew that once the council became involved they had the power to remove and destroy these unfortunate birds. The ball was in my court. 'Right!' I said.

Gulliver

'Nobody is going to destroy any birds while I am involved. I will take the chicks into my care and then the adult birds will leave the nest.' A practice which I do not condone but I felt on this occasion that there was no alternative.

The nest was situated between chimney-pots which rested on a very tall Victorian chimney-stack. Using ladders courtesy of the roofing boss I began to climb, and I could quite understand the feelings of the workmen as the parent herring gulls started trying to prevent me from reaching the nest. The view from the chimney-stack was quite breathtaking. To the north, I could see Scarborough Castle and beyond, and to the south, the magnificent cliffs towering above the beach at Reighton.

There was only one chick in the nest; it was quite fat and healthy and about two weeks old. The chick made no fuss when I removed it from the nest. I put it in my jumper and began my long descent to the street below; again the parent herring gulls tried to stop me.

I took Gulliver to my sanctuary where in the weeks to come he made a great impression on both myself and my helpers.

In my experience I have found that herring gulls are the easiest birds to rear and re-introduce into the wild. This is because they are scavengers and don't easily give up the will to live. They are very easy to feed because of their scavenging instinct. When they are as young as Gulliver cat food goes down very well for a few weeks, and then a diet of fish bits and left-overs from the human plate.

It was about two weeks before I allowed Gulliver to join the other rescued gulls because some of them were much larger and rather aggressive. Most of the gulls had been hand reared and I kept them in a very large paddock to allow them the freedom to fly away.

My policy with healthy youngsters was to feed them well for about six to eight weeks. I then gradually decreased their food supply to encourage them to fly further afield in search of food, thus making way for more refugees.

This method worked extremely well; I only wish it could have been used with hand reared owls and hawks, but that is another story.

Seal in Shop

My shop also doubled up as a base for my rescued animals. In some cases it was kinder for the sick and injured creatures to be treated and cared for at the shop rather than driving them several miles to my sanctuary.

There was always an air of excitement when someone appeared with a cardboard box. I would guide them to the rear of the shop and ask them what was in the box. They usually replied, 'It's a bird.' Sometimes inside an enormous box, wrapped in cotton wool I would find a young blue tit.

People also came to the sanctuary; one lady appeared carrying a box that once contained a television set. When I asked her what was inside, she replied, 'It's an eagle! It landed on my head.' I immediately donned my special gloves which I used for handling badgers and bad tempered Jack Russell terriers. Slowly I opened the box, removed the top flap and peered into the darkness below. There it was, a young kestrel. I could only assume that it had fallen from its nest just as the lady was passing by.

One morning a kindly gentleman brought a common seal pup into the shop. It was only a few weeks old and normally would still be relying on its mother's milk. My assistants immediately fell in love with this beautiful baby and were soon volunteering to feed it. I worked out a feeding programme and decided to keep the seal in the shop during the day so that there was always someone on hand to feed it. The food consisted of a mixture of goat's milk and liquidized fish, an evil smelling combination but the baby didn't seem to mind.

I was very lucky to know Alan and Brenda Giles who agreed to have my rescued seals at their West Norfolk Seal Rescue in Kings Lynn. I contacted them, hoping that they would have room for our baby seal. They said they were extremely busy treating dozens of seals which had a serious virus and felt it would wrong to put the seal pup at risk.

The shop always closed at four in the afternoon. Every day the same lady came in to browse through the second hand clothes racks five minutes before closing time. This particular day a volunteer had fed our baby and laid it under one of the circular, spin round clothes racks while she prepared to close for the day. True to form in walked the browsing lady at five to four. She began to browse through the clothes where our baby was resting. I came out of my office just at the same time as the browser lady let out a scream. 'There's a seal! There's a seal!' she cried. The seal, still feeling hungry, had come out from under the clothes rack and touched her feet. As she passed me on the way to the door she was still shouting, 'There's a seal!' I said something to the effect that we were trying to deal with the damp.

Needless to say the browser never returned. Our baby seal was eventually taken to The West Norfolk Seal Rescue and released three months later.

common seal pup

Humber Bridge Quandary

When I had rescued a seal I would contact Alan and Brenda and arrange to meet them at a specified time and place. We usually chose a very large car park on the approach to the famous Humber Bridge. This reduced the amount of travelling time for both parties. I must pay tribute to Alan and Brenda for their superb response in travelling to the rendezvous at any time day or night and sometimes in atrocious weather conditions. Truly dedicated people.

One one occasion we were in the middle of the car park with the two rescue vehicles and a very young but agile seal pup. It was about 2am and we were under one of the bright sodium lamps. I lifted the seal from my vehicle onto the ground and Alan prepared a syringe to inject the seal with antibiotics and multi-vitamins, whilst Brenda looked on. As Alan was about to inject the seal it slipped from my grasp and quickly slid under my vehicle. At that very moment two elderly people appeared in a car. When they saw me kneeling with a blanket over my arm, Alan with a large syringe and Brenda still looking on they drove away, did a couple of laps of the car park and then disappeared. Alan looked at me and said, 'I wonder what that was all about?' We proceeded to retrieve the seal for another injection attempt. As we were injecting the seal a Humber Bridge security van arrived with two security men inside. The van stopped several yards from us and they watched the injection taking place. After several minutes the security vehicle moved forward and the driver wound down his window and said, 'What's going on?' 'We are treating a rescued seal.' Alan replied. Satisfied with Alan's explanation they drove off. After the seal had been treated it was made comfortable, ready for the journey to Norfolk.

As we discussed the night's work we could not help laughing at how situations can be misinterpreted. The elderly couple wondered what three people were doing in the car park with a syringe and we wondered what an elderly couple were doing there at 2am. The two questions were never answered, or was it because they were never asked?

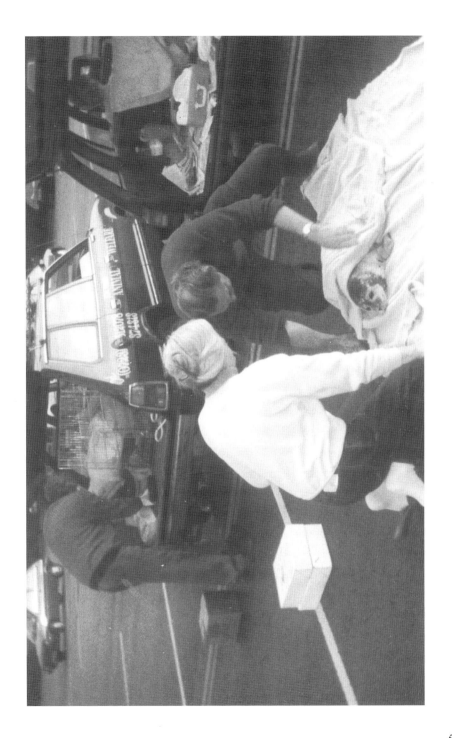

Otter and Otter

When the word 'otter' is mentioned I often wonder how many people think of the beautiful book, 'Ring Of Bright Water'. If only!

My mind springs back to when an irate garage owner rang me to say that two mad creatures were ransacking his stores. After a brief description I assumed they must be otters. I consoled the man and assured him that I was on my way. I arrived some twenty minutes later and was met by the man who pointed and shouted, 'They are in there!'

'There' was a large building which was used for storing spares. I slowly opened the door and peered in. The place was in a state of utter devastation. Large heavy storage racks were laid across the floor with cardboard boxes, washers, nuts and bolts etc. everywhere. In the middle of all the devastation were the two four-legged tornadoes. They were systematically emptying the boxes of their contents. They paused for a moment as I entered, looked at me, made a curious squeak and carried on with their vandalism. They were indeed otters, not English otters but Sumatran.

I retreated to the rescue vehicle still assuring the man that everything would be all right. He obviously had not seen the devastation. This particular rescue was in the early days of my wildlife adventures, so my equipment and certainly my knowledge of handling otters were limited. I checked my kit: two dog choke chains, one head collar for a pony, one pair of leather gloves and one large wicker basket for a cat or small dog. I put the gloves on, picked up the basket and strode past the man, who by now was sitting on a barrel with his head in his hands and making strange muttering sounds. The otters were still there but looking rather tired, or were they just preparing for the second half? I opened the basket and put it on the floor in one of the very rare clear spaces. Kneeling down beside the basket I made the 'click click' sound I used when calling my pet dog. To my surprise one of the otters responded and without hesitation ran very quickly towards me. Was I to hold my ground or retreat to the man sitting on the barrel? I held my ground.

The otter did not hesitate, it jumped onto my shoulder and proceeded to squeak and lick the top of my head and ears. Then without warning the otter started to explore my basket. Very quickly I shut the lid and fastened the straps. What a mistake! The otter started to scream and panic. Suddenly the other otter with teeth bared came running towards me and started attacking the basket. He then turned his attention on me; I say he because I found out later that the otter in the basket was his mate and in season. He attacked my legs several times and in doing so sprayed me with the most evil liquid I have ever smelled in all my life. After this onslaught he proceeded to destroy the basket and free his mate.

I returned to the man who was still sitting on the barrel. He stopped muttering and said, 'What's that smell?' I replied, 'It's me but it's not my fault! If you see what I mean.' He scratched his head. I explained the situation and I asked him if he had anything strong enough to contain two otters. 'I'll have a look,' he said, and disappeared into another building.

He quickly returned carrying a very large, square, metal container with a tap at the bottom. We soon found a substantial piece of plywood for a lid and a metal welding rod to fasten it. This time we both went into the stores. I carried the container and the man carried the lid. We strode over to the remains of the basket and I placed the container on the floor. The female otter immediately jumped into the container followed by her smelly mate. The man stood with his mouth wide open and I shouted, 'The lid! The lid!' On went the lid and we both sat on it and gave a sigh of relief. After making sure the otters were safe and secure we put the container into my rescue vehicle. I said goodbye to the man and said I hoped he would be able to sort out his stores.

On returning to Scarborough I had to walk several hundred yards to my office. People whom I knew well and who would normally stop and pass the time of day walked quickly away. When I arrived at my shop one of my volunteers greeted me with, 'What's that smell?' Again I replied, 'It's me!'

After taking a shower and putting my clothes in the bin I received a phone call from a man who was making enquiries about two tame Sumatran otters. Apparently they belonged to a lady who was abroad on holiday and were being cared for by this man. The lady's house had been burgled and the otters were accidentally set free.

I hope you will now realize why 'Ring of Bright Water' does nothing for me.

Collectable Heron

Running a wildlife rescue service and a fund raising shop had its difficulties. Sometimes there was a shortage of volunteers. Most of my helpers were housewives and mothers so it was impossible for them to work more than on a part-time basis which meant that sometimes I was alone in the shop.

On one such occasion I received a phone call from the curator of one of our local museums. He said that there was a heron standing near one of the ornamental ponds in the museum gardens and he was concerned because there were no fish in the pond and the heron had been there for several days.

I locked up the shop, making sure to leave the standard note on the door, 'Back in fifteen minutes'. I arrived at the museum to find the heron standing quite still near the pond. I knew if he had not eaten for several days he would be quite weak and it would not be too difficult to catch him. I slowly approached him saying my stock statement, 'Hello sweetheart. What are you doing here?' Someday I may get a reply; one which I could not repeat. There was very little response so I picked the heron up, making sure to point his spear-like beak in the opposite direction to my eyes. He did not struggle and I could feel how thin he was.

I returned to the shop and found a message on my answer machine saying that there was a pigeon trapped in an empty property on the outskirts of town. I put the heron on a table in my office and set off to release the pigeon. A task I quickly accomplished.

Again I returned to the shop and found a lady with a pleasant smile waiting on the doorstep. I passed the time of day with her and apologised for the shop being closed. She excused me, and then said, 'How much is the Capo di Monte figure in the window?' I hesitated for a few seconds and then said smilingly, 'I would be very fortunate if I had a Capo di Monte figure to sell.' The lady was adamant and pointing to the window said, 'There it is!' When I looked the heron was standing on one leg, still as a statue, looking into a large glass fruit bowl. I laughed and assured the lady that this was a real live heron which I had rescued earlier on in the day. The lady shrugged her shoulders and made off down the road, perhaps to look for the nearest opticians.

The heron was fed very well for the next few days, needless to say at my sanctuary and not the shop. I then successfully released him into a local heronry.

Permanent Guests

Many people who have been involved with animal sanctuaries will agree that it is very stressful seeing the suffering of dumb animals. It is also a fact that rescued animals receive careful nursing and in the case of my sanctuary, my patients were released back into the wild as quickly as it was possible to alleviate the stress of being in captivity.

Unfortunately, many rescued animals and birds cannot be released for various reasons: wings damaged beyond repair; young owls, because of their inability to hunt after being hand reared, become totally dependent on the hand that feeds them.

I had in my care many birds which could never be released because of their injuries. I tried to give them all some quality of life. I had four such birds in my care that I felt stood out above the rest. There was a gannet called Gannet, a wood-pigeon called Woodbine, a puffin called Pufkin and a European eagle owl called Nelson.

Gannet was rescued by a trawlerman several miles out at sea. He was quite young and had a very badly damaged wing which was beyond repair. After treatment by my vet he was introduced to the other inmates and settled in quite well. He certainly had an enormous appetite.

After a few weeks he was allowed the freedom of the sanctuary and would take advantage of this. He was into everything! He found out where I stored the fish and announced his presence with a large cackling sound and would attack the freezer with his large beak. On the occasions when I worked in the garden Gannet would follow me with a funny waddling walk which reminded me of Charlie Chaplin and then stand and watch me dig, with his beak nearly on the fork. Suddenly, he would stab his beak into the soil and pull out a worm which he promptly threw into the air. He repeated this action several times until boredom set in and then he wandered off to torment the herring gulls in the next paddock. Gannet lived happily with me for three years.

As stated, this chapter is about permanent guests; Pufkin, the puffin doesn't really qualify, but because of his enormous character I feel he deserves a mention. He was brought into my care after being totally immersed in crude oil. His chances of surviving were very slim indeed. Pufkin was so ill when he arrived at my sanctuary I decided not to try to remove the oil and I put him straight under a heat lamp for about four hours. I then pumped a mixture of cod liver oil and milk of magnesia into his stomach. This was a method I used on all oil polluted birds with some degree of success. The cod liver oil dislodges any oil which the bird may have ingested and the milk of magnesia lines the stomach which helps to stop the oil from burning.

After treating him I put Pufkin under the heat lamp for the night, fully expecting him to be dead the next day. To my surprise and delight he had survived the night and was standing and looking around at his new home. I knew the worst was to come; the cleaning process. I cleaned Pufkin and again put him under the heat lamp. There was nothing else I could do but wait and I said a few prayers for his recovery. My prayers were answered as Pufkin made a very remarkable recovery. I moved him into a small compound and he was soon eating white bait, a small fish very similar to sand eels which is the natural diet of puffins.

Pufkin flew away after only one week in my care. I knew this could prove fatal for him because in my opinion he was not quite

strong enough to fend for himself; he certainly was not water-proofed, but most importantly of all the sanctuary was several miles from the coast. He proved me wrong.

Two days after he had flown away Pufkin came back. This was truly unusual for this type of bird, also he was an adult bird and certainly had not been hand reared. This practice went on for several weeks. He would fly away and return after two to three days. I did, however, notice that he always returned when the weather was bad; perhaps the sand eels were more difficult to catch. Pufkin finally flew off and never returned. Such a little character with an enormous spirit, I wish him well.

Woodbine the wood pigeon also deserves a mention as he was a long term stay; he had fallen from his nest and I had to hand rear him. He became imprinted and was very protective towards me. He would fly onto my shoulder and attack anyone who came too near. This could be quite embarrassing when some sweet old lady was about to give me a donation. Woodbine carved himself a reputation at the sanctuary. He feared nothing and no one. He stayed with me for about three years and then one day, off he went. Perhaps to find a mate or to start a Third World War!

Last, but by no means least, Nelson. I do not believe that wild creatures should be bought and sold but, just once, I made an exception whilst visiting a falconry show. My attention was drawn to a very beautiful, young European eagle owl. You might say it was love at first sight. I felt so sorry for him because he was standing on a log with a chain tied to his leg. I approached the owner and asked if he would sell him to me and to my surprise he said in one breath,'Yes, he's a hundred pounds.' My only breath was to gasp, partly with relief and partly from shock at the mention of one hundred pounds. I accepted and agreed to collect Nelson the following week when I had raised the princely sum. I brought him to my sanctuary and I christened him Nelson because he had a small cataract on one eye. I knew I could give him a better quality of life even though he could never be released into the wild. I prepared an enormous flight cage with sleeping quarters the size of a very large dog kennel to enable him to stretch his enormous five foot wing span. I did quite a lot of research into eagle owls and found that the largest owl in the world, the great grey, is only slightly larger than the European eagle owl. I also discovered that Nelson would have been capable of killing a roe-deer in the wild. Through many generations of captive breeding Nelson was extremely placid and may I say, affectionate.

There followed a few months of constant contact during which Nelson and I enjoyed numerous trips into the local forest; we also enjoyed exploring the sea shore together, enabling us to create a very close bond with each other. He would travel in the back of my jeep perched on a log, which was eventually to go wherever Nelson and I went.

I was asked to take assembly at one of the local primary schools. This was my chance to take Nelson. I was rather reluctant to take any of my rescued wild birds because it would have been too stressful for them. The day came for me to go to the school and I arrived about thirty minutes before assembly. I met the headmaster and introduced him to Nelson. The look on the headmaster's face was priceless. With wide eyes he said, 'Good God! Is it safe?' After assuring him that Nelson loved children, but not to eat, I put his precious log on the speaker's table in the assembly hall along with my notes. I then retreated to a small room and waited for the children and teachers to assemble. The headmaster introduced me and I walked in with Nelson on my arm. I said, 'Good morning, I am Jim Ward and this is Nelson.' Nelson looked at me with his enormous orange eyes, turned and faced the assembly and promptly ruffled his feathers amidst a cloud of dust. There were roars of laughter from the children. It was at that moment I knew that Nelson would be a great success wherever he went. As I gave my talk that morning, I don't think many children heard much of what I was saying

because of some of the comic antics created by my huge feathered partner. After assembly the headmaster asked if the children could touch Nelson. I agreed. Almost every child in the school either stroked or cuddled him and he loved every minute of it.

As time went on, instead of walking onto the platform with Nelson, I instructed the headmaster to get all the children sitting in the assembly hall and announce that Mr Ward and his friend were going to give a talk. I entered through the door at the end of the hall with Nelson on my arm and I would hear all the gasps of 'Wows and Oohs,' coming from the children. I then released Nelson. He knew where his log was and would fly very low over the heads of the children and land on his log. I followed Nelson to the platform saying, 'Good morning children' and the children replied, 'Good morning.' I would then say, 'I'm Mr Ward and this is Nelson, say hello to Nelson.' He would turn his head and look into my eyes. It was more like a ventriloquist's act. Nelson knew what was needed of him.

Nelson's fame spread very quickly. We found ourselves travelling to many schools around North Yorkshire and into Hebden Bridge on the Lancashire border. We also appeared on television. Never once did Nelson let me down.

I wish the story of Nelson had a happy ending but sadly it does not. It saddens me even as I write. We were attending a small local boarding school and the talk, as ever, was a success. I was walking back to my jeep with Nelson on my arm when a driver of a delivery van slammed a door. Nelson turned his head very quickly striking me on the chin with his head. He staggered for a few seconds and then he seemed to be all right. When I returned to my sanctuary I knew all was not well with Nelson. I took him to the vet, Jane examined him and said he might be suffering from concussion. I cancelled the school visits which had already been booked to give Nelson time to recover. As the weeks went by Nelson's health deteriorated and I decided to take him to one of the most experienced bird vets in the country. He told me to leave Nelson with him and he would carry out some tests. I waited three days, three of the longest days of my life, the vet rang and asked me to collect dear

Nelson. He told me that there was a tumour at the base of Nelson's skull and sadly there wasn't anything he could do for him. I had to face the fact that Nelson would not recover. I brought him home and the following day took him to my vet who knew Nelson very well. Jane gave him a painless injection and we both shed some tears. Following his death I received many lovely letters from school children who knew Nelson. This somehow gave me the strength to carry on my rescue work in his memory.

Snowy

One of the birds I had the privilege to have in my care was a female snowy owl, rescued from a small local zoo which had unfortunately failed. I named her Snowy for obvious reasons. She was far from healthy when she came into my care. Also one of her wings was deformed so she was unable to fly but what she lacked in flight she certainly gained on the ground.

I brought her to my sanctuary and installed her in a specially prepared pen equipped with ramps. These would enable her to walk up to a platform where she could feed. It didn't take very long for Snowy to settle into her new home, in fact she became quite possessive. Unfortunately Snowy did not have a great deal of patience and she cornered me several times in her pen; not a bird to argue with. Her talons were quite lethal.

I had many visitors to the sanctuary and Snowy always drew a great of interest with her beautiful orange eyes and plumage like ermine. One day a photographer asked if he could photograph Snowy out of her pen, in surroundings which would look more natural. He assured me that he was a professional, and agreed to stop photographing Snowy when she showed signs of impatience. I put Snowy into her specially designed carrying case and proceeded to find a suitable spot in the nearby forest where I gave her exercise regularly. It didn't take me long to find a small clearing with patches of short grass and heather. I waited until the photographer had set up his equipment before I released Snowy. She immediately wandered over to a nearby rock and started to rearrange her feathers after her short journey.

The photographer was overjoyed to see this magnificent bird so relaxed, grooming herself. He said, 'This is amazing! What else does she do?' I, for once, was speechless. After several seconds I said, 'She doesn't do tricks.' Perhaps I should have said, 'She rides a bicycle.' It was after that question I began to doubt whether this man had ever photographed a bird of prey.

He took several of what he called distance shots, which was quite acceptable, but then he asked if he could take a close-up. By this time Snowy had stopped grooming and was watching her photographer. I knew she didn't want to eat him as she had already eaten

and photographers were never on Snowy's menu. My reply to his question was a very polite 'No' and warned him that Snowy was getting 'A LITTLE AGITATED.' 'Perhaps it would be possible if I crawled on my stomach?' I again said, 'NO' and began chuckling inwardly at my thoughts because he was a rather portly gentleman and certainly had a stomach to crawl on.

I decided that it was time to get Snowy's carrying case from my vehicle. After lifting it out, I turned round only to see Snowy's photographer crawling on his hands and knees within ten feet of her. 'Must have had second thoughts about using his stomach,' I mused. I dare not shout. I had to stand and watch what happened next. Snowy had fixed her sights on this strange object crawling towards her. She raised all her feathers as a warning to this figure but it kept on coming. Then, what I feared might happen, HAPPENED: she set up a terrifying screech which echoed through the forest. With talons outstretched she attacked; her screech was minimal compared to that let out by the photographer. He tried to run before he stood up, if you know what I mean. The camera went in one direction and the photographer tried to go in the other; only the camera was successful. Luckily, Snowy had made her point and returned to her stone. I waited half an hour or so before I attempted to return Snowy to her carrying case, the photographer keeping his distance.

When the three of us returned to the sanctuary I asked the photographer if he would like a cup of coffee. Needless to say he had been silent until then. He replied, 'No thank you, I must get back to the office.'

I have often wondered if that photographer gained any 'WILD UNDERSTANDING'!

Guest Speaker

To be the guest speaker at a function was one of the most pleasant tasks which went with my work and my involvement with the general public; it could be either at a posh dinner or at the local cub hut.

I was invited to give a talk on my wildlife rescue work to a combined group of cubs, gathered from several villages in the Scarborough and Whitby area. The talk was due to commence at 6.30pm but, unfortunately, I was called out to a rescue situation which made me rather late and I did not arrive until about 7pm. There was a packed village hall with around one hundred restless cubs and their leaders who seemed to be fast running out of patience. Usually I had the notes on my work in order but on this occasion everything was rather mixed up. Before I could explain this to the cub leader I was being introduced as the great wild life expert. As I looked across the hall I could see one hundred cubs with mouths open, waiting.

On the spur of the moment I said jokingly, 'Suck your thumbs whilst I sort out my notes.' Eventually I did sort out my notes. When I looked up again I saw one hundred cubs sucking their thumbs and the leaders looking on with faces full of confusion.

The talk proved to be a success and I'm sure there were quite a few converts by the time I left.

———

I recall one rather amusing talk to the Scarborough Townwomen's Guild. My subject on this occasion was about 'Birdigans', the woolly vests worn by the rescued sea-birds in my care that were suffering from the effects of oil pollution. The ladies seemed to enjoy my talk and the evening went very smoothly until question time. One poor lady who had completely missed my point on the subject asked if other birds ever attacked my birds when they were released wearing the jumpers. She left herself wide open to my sense of humour; I refrained, though I could have replied, 'It all depends on what colour the jumpers are. If there were eleven puffins wearing Liverpool colours and eleven guillemots wearing Arsenal colours on Bempton Cliffs at the same time there would be chaos.' OR 'The jumpers worn by migratory birds would need to have a pocket to house their passports.'

Luckily the chairperson intervened and gave our dear questioner a crash-course on polluted bird-care. However, there were quite a few titters.

Giving talks really did give me a sense of well-being and of course it strengthened my self-confidence. Above all it enabled me to meet some very interesting people.

Guest speaker at the Brompton-by-Sawdon WI meeting on the 20th January 1999 in the village hall.

An Evening's Howl

I had a request to give a talk to the Stamford Bridge Watch Group. The talk was to be entitled, 'An Owl Evening.' As a special treat I decided to take three of my tame owls. They were tame because they had been hand reared at my sanctuary.

The date for the booking arrived and I knew I had to be away from the sanctuary that day as I was extremely busy with various rescues and, of course, releases. During the day I realized that I would be short of time when I got back to the sanctuary and the talk was to begin at 7pm. I decided to ring my assistant and instruct her to put one barn owl, one tawny owl and a little owl into separate carrying baskets. This would save some considerable time as Stamford Bridge was some thirty miles from Scarborough.

All went according to plan. I collected my ready packed owls and set off for my destination. I arrived in the village of Stamford Bridge at around 6.45pm. There were quite a few people walking along the road and as it was dark I stopped to ask someone if they could direct me to the village school. He obligingly pointed me in the right direction and then asked me if I too were going to the Owl Evening. I assured him that I was and carried on. We arrived at the school which was much larger than I expected and people seemed to be coming from every direction. The playground was being used as a car park and the attendant directed me to a parking space at the rear entrance. I went inside and a very friendly gentleman introduced himself as the headmaster. He took me into a little room at the end of the assembly hall. I told the headmaster that I would leave the owls in this room until I had given my talk and then I would display them. The headmaster introduced me to the leader of the Watch Group and departed. He seemed delighted with the turn-out and invited me to peep through the curtain, which I did. I froze. My knee caps started to go up and down like high speed yo-yos. There were literally hundreds of people; there were cameras; there were gift and craft stalls.

I asked the Watch Group leader where all these people had come from. He replied that they came from York and surrounding villages. He then explained that I had become very popular because some of my stories had been on local BBC radio. Was I to stay popular?

The time came for the Watch Group leader to introduce me and I stepped onto the stage to loud applause which drowned the sound of my knocking knees. Once I started speaking everything fell into place and the audience appeared to be listening with interest. There were gurgling sounds occasionally coming from some of the very young children, but on the whole they were a very well behaved lot. I told a few stories of funny rescues and tried to stay clear of the sad ones. The talk lasted for about an hour, followed by a fifteen minute interval after which I came back to answer questions. Then I sprang my surprise. The leader of the Watch Group was about to give his vote of thanks when I gave a pre-arranged signal to my assistant and she brought in the carrying baskets. The first owl I took out was my favourite barn owl, an absolutely magnificent bird and a total show off. There was plenty of 'Oohs' from the females in the audience. I spoke for a few minutes about this particular owl before putting it back in its basket. Next should have been a very tame tawny owl but for some reason the wrong bird had been put in the basket. I did not know I would be handling a very wild aggressive bird which had only been in my care for a few days after being in collision with a car.

As I inserted my unprotected hand into the basket I was greeted with a very loud scream from within. I then felt extreme pain in the back of my hand and at the end of a finger. There were gasps from the audience who, I suspect, thought this was part of the show until I withdrew my hand from the basket with a very angry tawny owl still attacking it. By the time I managed to get the bird off my hand and back into the basket there was quite a lot of blood around.

The Watch Group leader arrived with a tea cloth and wrapped the wounds whilst the speaker was trying to explain to the audience that he had intended to let the children handle the owls but it would not be wise in view of what had happened.

Apart from that unexpected incident the evening went quite well. I still cannot answer why the wild tawny owl did not attach itself to my assistant when she put him into the basket at the sanctuary. Maybe the journey to Stamford Bridge had upset him?

An Arresting Thought

The majority of my rescued sea birds were understandably aggressive and therefore difficult to handle.

Guillemots, puffins and razor-bills spend most of their lives out at sea and to survive, as I stated earlier, need to be perfectly waterproof. Unfortunately, due to oil pollution, many come ashore and have to be rescued by people like myself.

Another bird which spends most of its life in water is a cormorant. Their waterproofing is not as efficient as the birds previously mentioned. They can be seen standing on rocks, buoys, boats and sea walls flapping and outstretching their wings allowing them to drip-dry.

The cormorant is on my list of not so friendly birds. They have a very sharp, small hook on the tip of their beak and they dig it into your flesh, inflicting a nasty gash. I have rescued many cormorants and I always treated them with the greatest respect. I was once called to our local police station to collect a cormorant which had bitten a boy, causing him a facial injury. The poor lad had to be taken to hospital to have it stitched. He had seen the bird on a rock and made the mistake of thinking that the bird was in distress. He had walked up behind the cormorant, thrown a towel over it and struggled home. While he was transferring the bird from the towel to a box it had attacked him. I arrived at the police station and the desk constable said, 'It's in that little broom cupboard and it's got out of the box.' I noticed that on the floor in front of the reception desk there was quite a lot of blood, and I said, 'Oh goodness me! Is the cormorant injured?' He said, 'No,no, it isn't the cormorant's blood. It's the duty sergeant's. The cormorant bit him and he's had to go to hospital.' I put on my protective gloves, opened the door, went inside, and there was the cormorant, waiting. He was naturally very upset; he'd attacked the boy, he'd attacked the duty sergeant and I was the next candidate.

When he did attack me he took me by surprise because I wasn't expecting him to go for my leg. He grabbed the inside of one of my calves. Luckily my trousers cushioned the impact and I was able to unhook him. I had to wrestle with him in order to get him into a carrying case and I thought, 'I must look like Roy Hull with Emu.'

Ups and Downs

We have all heard of someone having their ups and downs. I for one have had just that, quite literally. Many times I have been called out to a rescue which was either up a cliff or down a cliff, never along. I have often wondered if I added together the amount of feet I climbed in twenty years of rescue, would I be able to reach the moon?

In Scarborough a number of years ago at the harbour end of the Marine Drive contractors were building a sewage pumping station. The cliffs at the back of the station are very high and very steep and every spring a large colony of kittiwakes come to use them for nesting. The contractors had to put a large net against the cliff face to stop boulders falling onto the site offices below. When the kittiwakes arrived from their winter out at sea most of them were unable to settle on the ledges. A few managed to get behind the net but were unable to find their way out. Members of the public soon saw what was happening and called upon my services. I was officially recognized by the local rescue services so I was able to put a rescue plan into operation by asking the fire service for assistance. They arrived very promptly with a turntable ladder which unfortunately was about fifty feet too short. I thanked the firemen for their support knowing that it was now up to me to rescue the trapped kittiwakes.

I rang Carolyn, who was a good friend and willing helper. I explained the situation and the reason why this rescue needed two people. One person to remove the trapped birds and one to hold the hessian bag which would keep the birds safe on the return journey down the cliffs. I asked for her help. There was a pause at the other end of the phone and I thought she might have collapsed at the prospect of climbing up the sheer cliffs. I didn't really believe that because I knew she was quite a spirited lady.

Carolyn and I arrived at the site armed with gloves and the hessian sack. It was very windy but thankfully dry. We had to climb up a very steep, sixty foot grassy bank before we reached the net. It was very hard on our leg muscles and we certainly needed a rest before starting the final assault. We looked out across Scarborough's North Bay. We must have had the best view in Scarborough but I certainly wouldn't recommend seeing it from this vantage point.

We eventually started to climb the net which was quite difficult because of the strong winds. We were swaying backwards and forwards, not a word was spoken and I thought at one stage we must have looked like Spiderman and Spiderwoman. Sadly the first two birds we came across were dead due to starvation. We successfully managed to rescue four very weak birds and after they had been fed for a couple of days they were ready to be released.

The contractors, having witnessed two determined people climbing their net to rescue trapped birds, decided to cover it with one that had a much smaller mesh. Both nets were removed some months later when the site opened.

As for Carolyn I will always be indebted to her and her courage and I'm sure the kittiwakes will.

Carolyn with Spook and Spectre (barn owls)

THAT WAS THE UP; NOW FOR THE DOWN.

I have watched over and over again and marvelled at the beauty of kittiwakes, puffins, gannets, fulmars to name but a few, as they soar close to the cliffs on the air currents. It is of course a different story when a bird becomes trapped in fishing line half way down a four hundred foot cliff face.

I was once called out to such an incident which meant abseiling down the cliff to rescue a trapped fulmar. This was the first time I had been involved with a fulmar but I knew for certain that if I got too close it would try to bite my hand or at worst my nose. So with gloves on hands and heart in mouth I started my descent. I lowered myself so that I was just below the bird and then hauled myself up to a working position opposite the fulmar and said, 'Hello Sweetheart, I'll soon have you loose.'

The words were no sooner out of my mouth when the fulmar made a noise like a grunting pig and proceeded to squirt an evil smelling liquid at me. It could only be described as rotting fish. He scored a direct hit and got me full in the face. I wiped off the excess with my sleeve and using my knife managed to cut the fishing line from around the bird's legs. After putting the bird into a hessian bag I wound up the remaining line to dispose of later. I started the long haul back up the cliffs. When I got to the cliff-top I gave the bird a thorough examination and was delighted to find that it hadn't received any injuries. I released it immediately and gave him back his freedom.

I researched the habits of fulmars and discovered that they squirt liquid purely as a natural defence mechanism. Pity I didn't do that beforehand!

Seal of Approval

One of the most difficult creatures I have been called upon to rescue are seals. Perhaps it is because they always choose to come ashore in the most inaccessible places when ill or injured, such as the base of a two hundred foot cliff, or on rocks covered with seaweed; or was it just the fact that seal pups are aero-dynamically like a four stone live sausage? Adults are just the same only heavier. However, I was called to a seal pup which contradicts the statement I have just made.

Filey is an unspoilt, sleepy fishing town with its own special 'feel'. It welcomes visitors and they love to come to relax and unwind.

I collected my assistant and drove the six miles along the coast road. We arrived in Filey at 11.30pm and found the seal on the steps which lead to the promenade. There were several onlookers who were keeping their distance. I approached with caution. I wanted to try to find out what had caused him to come ashore. When I was within touching distance I discovered that he was sleeping quite soundly and rather than touch him I said, 'Hello.' That was my first mistake because he leapt three feet in the air and immediately retreated to a very deep pool under the sea wall. It was quite obvious that the seal was not in any trouble but had been merely resting and the tide had left him high and dry. I decided that I could not leave him in the pool as there was a danger of dogs attacking him. That was my second mistake.

I put my wellies on and proceeded to send the seal to the seaward end of the pool. The seal had other ideas. He started to swim in very small circles around me until my wellies were full of water. He was really enjoying himself and still not quite satisfied. When I was in the centre of the pool he head butted the rear of my legs and I landed flat on my back, totally submerged. When I surfaced I heard the roar of laughter coming from my assistant and the onlookers. I remember remarking, 'You lot should be at home in bed at this time of night!'

While I regained my composure the seal quite happily made his way down the beach, back to the sea, perhaps to tell the rest of the colony of how he had ducked a human being.

Oh Lucky Tim

A deeply distressed lady arrived at my door with a fox cub wrapped in an anorak. The poor creature had a serious rear leg injury and he was very wet and very cold. The lady said that she had found the cub stuck between two rocks at the foot of some steep cliffs whilst searching for fossils. The tide was coming in and he would have drowned if she had not found him. I could only assume that the six week old fox cub had fallen over two hundred feet from the cliff-top.

The lady insisted that a vet should be consulted and said that she would pay for the treatment no matter what it cost. I assured her that I would have consulted the vet as this was normal procedure. We took the cub to the surgery and an X-ray showed that the bone in the leg was shattered. The vet advised us to have the cub put to sleep but the lady said the cub must be given a chance. The vet agreed to operate and said to ring her the following afternoon. When I rang the vet told me that she had repaired the shattered bone with several small pins which held it together.

I arrived at the surgery to collect the cub and when I returned home I rang the lady to give her the good news. There was a few seconds of silence and then in a tearful voice she thanked me for all my help. She visited the cub every Sunday and brought him food and she christened him Tim.

After about six weeks Tim was much larger and livelier. It was time to have the pot removed to see if the pins had done their job. The vet told me that there was a possibility of muscle wastage due to the fact that the leg had not been used for six weeks. The leg was X-rayed again and the bone had healed perfectly due to the young age of the cub. The vet said she would not remove the pins as there would be no ill effects. For several days after the removal of the pot Tim seemed reluctant to put his injured leg onto the ground. This did not stop him romping with my dog and cat. As time went on the leg muscle grew stronger and it was difficult to tell there had been an injury. The months passed by very quickly and the lady continued to visit and it was so wonderful to see how happy she was when she was with Tim. Unfortunately my health began to deteriorate and I knew that in the near future I would have to go into hospital for treatment. This meant that I had to find alternative accommodation for my patients. It would not be difficult to rehouse the birds and small mammals but at that time it was difficult to find sanctuaries that catered for foxes and larger mammals. Fortunately after discussing the problem with Tim's rescuer I found a sanctuary that agreed to take him, and it was just twenty miles from my home. I hoped I would be able to take Tim back within a few weeks.

The treatment wasn't a success so I had to leave Tim at the sanctuary. The owner decided to release Tim from his enclosure, giving him the freedom to roam around her fifteen acre property which included a wooded area. I didn't worry because he usually came back to his foster home in the evening and food was left out for him. He kept returning for several months. Eventually his visits ceased so I could only hope that he had found a mate to share his freedom.

Drunk in Charge of a Seal

I decided to have an early night after a extremely busy day. I lay reflecting on what I had to do the following day when the ringing of the phone interrupted my thoughts. It was the local police informing me that there was a stranded seal pup on the foreshore beach at Scarborough, and they were concerned for the seal's safety.

I contacted my assistant, picked her up and off we went to find the seal. When we arrived there were quite a few people about on the seafront. I drove my jeep onto the beach and switched on the searchlight. I had been driving very slowly for about two hundred yards when I saw a very large dark object. I stopped, looked, and said to my assistant, 'That's not a seal pup, it's far too big!' I climbed out of the jeep and started to walk towards the object. I was about six feet away when I realized that the object was a man. He was lying full length on the sand with one arm round a very small seal pup, and in his other hand he had a piece of fish with batter on. He was trying to share his supper with the seal pup. I could hear him saying in a very slurred voice, 'You're all right pal, Jim Ward won't be long.' I gently removed our drunken hero's arm and carried my rather confused patient to the jeep. As I drove back to the sanctuary my assistant said, 'What about the drunk?' I replied, 'Don't worry. The tide's coming in.'

I did, however, inform the police of the drunk's location, and I was pleased that everything had gone smoothly, but a bit sorry because I didn't get my early night.

I have often wondered what the drunk's friends thought when he tried to explain the story of the disappearing seal. Perhaps he had better stick to pink elephants.

Never Kiss a Macaw

I was just finishing my meal on a very warm Sunday afternoon when I received a call from the local police. A valuable macaw had gone missing.

They gave me the telephone number of the lady owner whom I duly rang. Amidst tears and sobs the lady explained because it was such a lovely day she had decided to let her pet macaw, Charlie, stand on his T-shaped perch on the lawn. She thought he could not fly away because his wings had supposedly been clipped. He must have decided that this chance was too good to miss, so he flew onto a small tree and from there he just took off. Scarborough is not exactly the Amazon jungle, or even the next best thing, but it was good enough for this bird. The lady with the help of friends had spent hours looking for Charlie; eventually he was spotted quite near his home resting in a sycamore tree. After several minutes of macaw owner psychology I managed to reassure the lady I would do all in my power to recover her beloved pet. I told her it would be useless to try to catch the bird so shortly after it had gained its freedom. My plan was to keep an eye on Charlie until he decided to settle down for the night and then carry out my rescue.

I put my twenty foot extending ladder onto my car's roof rack and off I went to the scene. A small crowd had gathered to watch the rescue. I looked up at the mature eighty foot sycamore and spotted Charlie perched on one of the upper branches.

Charlie's owner waited in her home, too scared perhaps to see the bird fly away again and disappear forever. It seemed like days waiting for dusk. After several cups of tea the moment arrived and I put my ladder onto the first branch. I was on my own, up I went into the darkness wondering what I would do if the bird flew away before I could capture him, and then having to report my failure to the poor lady waiting at home. As I neared the top of the tree the branches got thinner and more unstable; even so I managed to get within fifteen feet of Charlie before I decided it was far too dangerous to continue. A decision which I should have made before making the long climb. When I reached the ground I asked the lady who was making the cups of tea if I could ring the police; she agreed over another cup of tea.

I explained the situation to the police and they asked me what could they do to help. I said it would be extremely helpful if they could contact the fire brigade for me and ask for their assistance. Within minutes they arrived with a recently acquired machine for lifting two persons to a great height and a stem light, which is a telescopic apparatus with a bright light at the top. The crowd got bigger. Perhaps somebody would turn up with a hot dog stall? The pressure was beginning to tell on me. What if I lost the bird in front of such a large crowd? The station officer asked where I wanted the equipment positioning and told me that I was in charge. I asked the officer who would be operating the stem light to position the stem within fifteen feet of Charlie, but not to switch on the light until I gave the word. I clambered into the bucket with the fireman who was to operate the up, down and sideways levers. Once more into the darkness but this time not alone and feeling rather more secure. We stopped just beneath Charlie, within reaching distance of him, and I could just see Charlie's tail. There was absolute silence. I shouted, 'Lights' and the whole area was totally illuminated. I grabbed Charlie's tail hoping I would dislodge him from his perch so that I could grab hold of his neck with my other hand. However, I got the elbow of the hand which was going to grab Charlie's neck stuck in the rail around the bucket, so this meant that I pulled him off the branch with the hand which was around Charlie's tail. He spun round and grabbed my little finger with a beak that can crack a walnut and I felt the bone crack and saw the blood. I managed to free my elbow, prise Charlie's beak from my finger and grab the back of his neck and Charlie screamed. I have never ever heard a scream like it in all of my life. I think you could have heard it over the whole of North Yorkshire I shouted to the fireman to get me down as quickly as possible. When we reached ground level the crowd cheered and I received many pats on my back. As I put Charlie into the carrying box he said, 'Give us a kiss.' Having witnessed what he had done to my finger I declined.

I returned Charlie to his owner who rewarded me with a cash donation for having returned her treasured pet. My biggest reward was the look of sheer delight on the lady's face. Again Charlie said to me, 'Give us a kiss.' This time I obliged. I said a fond farewell and went to the hospital. The doctor confirmed that my finger was broken, and said it would need several stitches.

Back Seat Driver

One late summer evening I was contacted by the local coastguard. Two gentlemen who were on holiday had spotted a seal with a large cut on its neck. When I arrived on the scene at Primrose Valley the two gentlemen were waiting for me and I introduced myself. I explained to them what I intended to do.

The tide was out and the seal was a considerable distance from the sea which was to my advantage. The object was to secure a blanket around the head of the seal. Sounds simple; it is not! The seal was a Farne Islands grey, as I mentioned earlier they are noted for being very aggressive. This fellow was a first year bull and injured. I reassured the two gentlemen that seal rescues were quite a regular occurrence for me. I said that I would require their assistance when I was ready to lift the seal into my rescue vehicle because it weighed somewhere in the region of ten stone.

After about fifteen minutes and a lot of sand dancing I secured the blanket around the seal's head. The three of us finally managed to get the seal into a large circular fibreglass container. This had an open top so I secured a net over it and we lifted it into the back of the vehicle. I thanked the two gentlemen, shook hands with them and set off along the beach in my Subaru estate doing approximately four miles per hour. It had 'WILDLIFE RESCUE' in bold white lettering across the bonnet with a puffin as a logo. There was an amber light on the roof which I always used, especially on a beach where there were members of the public. As I made my way along the beach I noticed a young gentleman jogging towards Filey; apart from him the beach was deserted.

Everything seemed to be going quite well until I looked in the rear view mirror and saw to my horror the seal's head appearing over the back of my seat. It had somehow managed to get out of the container. I could feel his breath and most certainly smell it! There was no time to go through the driving test procedure of brakes, put into neutral and hand brake on. This wasn't a driving examiner but a very angry seal which wanted the back of my head. My only way out of this situation was to open the door and roll out on to the sand. Some people would call it cowardice, I called it survival. By the time I regained my feet the vehicle was still travelling and going towards the young jogger who was unaware of what was going on behind him. The seal must have thought that the windscreen was his only means of escape so he draped himself across the steering wheel and in doing so started to operate the horn. The jogger, hearing the commotion, turned round and saw a vehicle with 'Wildlife Rescue' on the bonnet, a flashing orange light and a seal behind the wheel. The jogger immediately turned into a sprinter.

I caught up with the vehicle and luckily for me the seal slipped onto the floor at the passenger side so I opened the door and switched off the ignition. The two gentlemen who assisted me had been watching the events from a distance. They came up to me and enquired, 'What was all that about?' I jokingly replied that I was giving the seal a driving lesson and he was so eager he pushed me out because he thought he could manage by himself.

The story did have a happy ending. After a short stay at The West Norfolk Seal Rescue the seal was released in The Wash.

May

I think without any fear of contradiction that the badger is one of Britain's best loved mammals. The badger is not seen by many people but it somehow depicts a true British creature; not an import, but something which has been with us since the beginning. Not all people are as warm to badgers as myself and millions of others. They are thankfully in the minority. I am speaking about the barbarians who follow their grisly pastime of badger baiting, not even fearful of the penalties imposed on them if they are caught. I will reserve my comments on the subject of penalties.

I have taken into my care many badgers; some have been victims of road accidents, others suffering from injuries, cause unknown, but one can only guess. One very young badger was brought into me by a motorist who had found it at the side of the road in a countryside location, a few miles from Scarborough. How the baby got there was a mystery; I could only make an assumption. The badger, a female, was about three weeks old, her eyes were barely open. She was certainly the youngest badger to be put into my care and my wonderful volunteers took it in turns to bottle feed her quite frequently. I have always found that goat's milk worked wonders and our baby was no exception. Incidentally, because she was found in May I christened her May. Quite original? I thought, ah well perhaps not.

May grew and grew and within six weeks she became quite a handful. She wanted to play when everyone wanted to sleep. She evicted my cat from his treasured basket and even used his litter tray and his cat flap. At the time I lived near Filey, in a very picturesque hamlet named Primrose Valley. It is very peaceful and the houses meander in tiers down to the cliff-tops. It has a busy holiday village on its doorstep which is very popular with families. I would think that the main reason for this is the four mile stretch of creamy white sand. May often walked along the beach with yours truly and my Alsatian, Max. What an unusual trio, but never mind; I felt quite normal. I remember one July evening; it was nearly dusk, and I decided to take May for a walk along a quiet lane close to home. I thought it was about the right time to teach her how to forage for slugs in the hedge bottom. So on my hands and knees with May beside me and my head pointing into an elderberry bush I started to make snuffling noises to get her interested.

Suddenly I heard a child's voice behind me saying, 'Mummy, what is that man doing?' Mummy replied, 'Come along darling, he thinks he's a badger!'

The time was coming very close to when May should be introduced back into the wild. It is recommended that five months is the age for release. Unfortunately young badgers cannot be released into a strange sett because the other badgers would certainly attack and kill the stranger, so the release procedure is quite complicated. In May's case I contacted the local Badger Protection Group, who in turn contacted the Forestry Commission, who created a simulated sett using suitable concrete pipes which were buried to make a tunnel leading to a central chamber. They used bedding from an established sett to spread around the simulated sett to give the new tenant, in this case May, the feeling of being at home. A low voltage electric fence would be put round the new home when she was installed to keep May in and any unwanted guests out. Regular supplies of food would be given to May for about three weeks, then the electric fence would be removed and May would be able to come and go as she pleased. Sounds simple, but it proved not to be.

The release date was fixed and I was getting uptight at having to part with my five-month-old bundle of dynamite, when a message came through; a local farmer had found a young male badger which was quite ill and very much under weight. He needed to be taken to a vet for treatment, also the Badger Protection Group would monitor him until he reached his normal weight.

It was decided to postpone May's release until the other badger could be released at the same time so that they would be introduced to their new home together. The farmer volunteered to keep his rescued badger in one of his barns. It wasn't long before the badger had recovered and had put on enough weight. I had mixed feelings about introducing May to her new mate, perhaps I felt I was losing her affection. Yes, even a badger can show that, but not May's new mate because he certainly didn't take kindly to humans. When I arrived at the farm with May he was in a sort of an arena made from bales of straw, something like a Roman Colosseum. Believe me I felt as if I was being thrown to a lion. The aggression he was showing was unbelievable until he saw May, and then his whole attitude changed; it was love at first sight. I left them together and I did not see May again.

After liaising with the Badger Protection Group I contacted the forest ranger and informed him that there were now two badgers ready for release, but when he checked the simulated sett he found that a family of badgers were already squatting in there. All was not lost; another sett was created and I am pleased to say that both our babies settled in quite well.

My close contact with such a young badger taught me so much about their habits, their likes and dislikes. She taught me what to expect from my next badger rescue and to gain a little more about that 'Wild Understanding.'

The Rott Set In

In the main, my role in life was to rescue wild creatures but on the odd occasion I was called out to rescue a domestic animal.

One very hot summer's day I received a telephone call from a security man who worked at one of the holiday villages near Scarborough. He said that a Rottweiler had been left in a tourer caravan and was suffering because of the intense heat.

At this time Rottweilers were receiving a great deal of bad publicity because there had been several reports of children in different parts of the country being attacked by this breed of dog. I appreciated the seriousness of the situation and arrived as quickly as I could. The senior security man pointed to the caravan, and before I could make any comments a police sergeant and a constable arrived. The sergeant walked a little way towards the caravan, pondered for a few seconds and then walked back to me, and said, 'Right Jim! What are we going to do?' I knew what he really meant, and that was, 'What are YOU going to do?'

I asked for an urgent message to be put out over the tannoy system for the owner of the dog to come and release it. No one came. I asked the senior security man to fetch a duplicate key for the caravan as quickly as possible. He opened the door, and as I prepared myself the Rottweiler lunged at the large window at the far end of the caravan, taking the whole pane of glass, window frame and curtains with her. She landed unharmed on the grass, ran through a hedge and down a busy main road in the direction of Scarborough.

We gave chase, me in my rescue vehicle, followed by a panda car, and at the rear the camp security vehicle. The convoy had followed the frightened Rottweiler for about a quarter of a mile when it suddenly ran into the garden of a detached bungalow. The convoy came to a halt and the pursuers peered over the fence that surrounded the garden. The Rottweiler was lying down in the middle of the lawn and panting very heavily. The sergeant put his hand on my shoulder and said,'What are you going to do now, Jim?' My answer could have been, 'I'm going home,' but, not being a defeatist, I answered, 'I'm going to capture it!'

I put into action a method which I sometimes used when rescuing a seal. I slowly started to crawl on my stomach towards the Rottweiler, not looking directly at it because having eye contact would mean I was a threat. When I was within touching distance I began to speak in a very soft voice, 'Come on sweetheart, you are safe now,' along with many of my other stock relaxing sayings. I slowly put my hand close enough for me to gently touch the Rottweiler and was rewarded with a very wet lick. I had made a new friend.

The dog was soon reunited with her owners who were very relieved to have her back. They did not realize that they were guilty of gross mistreatment of their family pet which could have resulted in the animal's death. I'm quite sure that they did not make the same mistake again.

Not My Seal of Approval

The phone rang just as I was settling down after Christmas dinner. It was the duty sergeant at our local police station. 'Sorry to trouble you, Jim. A gentleman visiting relatives for Christmas has spotted a seal trapped in a net at the bottom of some cliffs not far from Scarborough.' I knew the location quite well and assured the sergeant that I would attend, and wished him a Merry Christmas. I set off on the short journey equipped with my seal rescue equipment, not knowing that this rescue would nearly end in tragedy.

I met the gentleman about half a mile from the cliffs. There was only a narrow footpath and as we walked I explained the procedure of rescuing and handling a seal. It was dusk. I was carrying a very powerful lamp, to be used to dazzle the seal so that I could wrap it in a blanket, firstly covering the seal's head and then its whole body and finally tying the blanket with strong cord. This process is usually quite easy to do on land but I did not know I would have to carry it out on this occasion in the sea.

We arrived at the cliffs which were eighty to a hundred feet high, not totally sheer with quite wide ledges. The seal was on an outcrop of rock about fifty yards from the cliff face and it was wrapped up in strong fishing net which was also wedged in between jagged rocks. The tide was coming in but luckily the sea was quite calm. After giving the man instructions to shine the bright light into the seal's eyes I started to walk towards the seal. The water was above my knees and rising slowly by the time I reached it and I could see it was a grey seal, possibly from the Farne Islands. When he saw me he started to growl and I once again told my helper to keep the light directly on the seal's eyes.

I cut the net away from the rocks which only took several minutes, but it seemed like hours. By this time the water was above my waist, so as quickly as I could I wrapped the blanket around the seal. I had seen a very large gash in his neck, so I knew I would not be able to release him.

With quite a lot of effort, part wading and part swimming, I managed to secure the blanket with the cord. I began making my way to the cliffs and preparing myself for the long climb ahead. Suddenly a hole appeared in the blanket and at that moment everything went wrong. My helper, still with the lamp in his hand suddenly pointed it at me and shouted to tell me that the seal's head was free. I was blinded immediately, but the worst was to come because now the seal could see me. He launched a vicious attack to my face which unbalanced me and I became submerged still holding onto the cord. As I surfaced the seal struck again, this time with some success. I felt his teeth sink into my chin and again I found myself submerged. I ingested quite a lot of water and when I surfaced I was totally disorientated but luck was on my side. I saw that I was facing in the right direction and my feet were on solid rock. In sheer desperation I shouted to my helper rather angrily to shine the light on the seal and not me. I wrapped the blanket around the biting end of the seal, more by good luck than management and dragged him to the base of the cliffs. Before the gentleman and I started to climb we removed the net from the seal so that he would not be subjected to any more injuries and again I wrapped him in the blanket.

It took us nearly two hours to climb up the cliffs carrying the seal and then take him to my rescue vehicle. When I reached the sanctuary I made arrangements to have the seal collected by the West Norfolk Seal Rescue the next day. I then had to go to Scarborough hospital, casualty department, who knew me well, and have my chin stitched. The doctor told me it could have been more serious if the bite had been a few inches lower.

The seal was released some days later after having stitches too

Eye Eye

When you are dealing with most wild creatures bites are an every-day occurrence. Seals seem to make a hobby of trying to remove their rescuer's fingers. Herons like to try and poke out an eye or two. Puffins use a more subtle approach, they just grab your finger and hold it while applying pressure, something resembling a vice. While you try to take precautions against such injuries, accidents can happen and often do.

Gannets are Britain's largest sea birds with a wing span of over five feet. Their food intake is enormous; they can devour several pounds of mackerel a day. One adult male gannet had lost its way because of foggy conditions and landed on a busy main road near Scarborough. A quick thinking motorist used her car's hazard warning lights to protect the bird. The gannet refused to move despite attempts by members of the public to remove it from the road for its own safety; one man tried to use his umbrella as a prod, and this was quickly destroyed. I had been called out by the police and when I arrived with my large carrying box and strong gloves the police were already at the scene directing the traffic. After several minutes of wrestling and nifty footwork the gannet was safely tucked away and the traffic was able to get back to normal.

On examining the bird I found he had a slight dislocation of one of his wings, so would require some veterinary treatment and several weeks rest. He never really adapted to his new surroundings and would attack anyone who went too close, even when giving him food. The day came for me to take the gannet to Bempton Cliffs where Britain's largest mainland nesting colony breed. I took the precaution of wearing strong gloves and made sure I was holding the gannet's neck just in case he tried to stab my face with his powerful spear-like beak. Everything was going to plan and I was just about to put him into the carrying basket when I tripped. To save myself I let the gannet go but in doing so I fell close enough for him to stab my left eye with his beak.

My assistant took me to the casualty department at the local hospital where it was discovered that the gannet's beak had almost removed my eyelid and my eye ball was badly bruised. After a lot of painful probing the surgeon stitched my eyelid and I had to wait several days until the bruising had subsided to see if there would be a permanent injury to my eye. I was lucky!

I did not wave a friendly goodbye to the gannet on his release and I certainly did not want to keep an eye out for him!

Out to Bat

As a wildlife rescuer I was on twenty four hour call out to the local police and rescue services, so I never knew what time the phone would ring day or night.

One such call came at two o'clock in the morning. An elderly lady had reported a bat flying around in her bedroom. I responded immediately to find a very frightened lady in her lounge, refusing to enter her bedroom until the intruder had been removed. I went into the bedroom assuring the lady that I would find the bat and remove it for her. This type of rescue was quite routine; first I checked the creases in the curtains, an ideal place for these creatures to hide. I drew a blank. I then moved items of furniture,looked under the bed, checked the light fitting but there wasn't a sign of the bat. I assumed that the bat was a pipistrelle, small enough to hide in very limited spaces. With this in mind I started to look in less obvious places, like underneath the door; still no bat, no sounds or droppings. At this stage I returned to the lady and tried to reassure her, but she insisted that there was a bat. She was adamant and said she would not sleep in that room until it had been removed. After several cups of weak tea the lady decided to sleep in the spare room. I told her to ring me straight away if she saw the bat again.

Two days later and again at two in the morning, yes, you've guessed, the lady and her bat. She told me that it was now flying around in the spare room. I went again and spent a long time searching but I did not find it. So reluctantly, again I had to leave a very distressed elderly lady.

In the meantime I found out that the lady lived in sheltered accommodation. I went to see the warden who informed me that the lady had a fixation about bats and was having treatment at the local psychiatric hospital.

I was of course ready for the third call and arrived at the lady's flat armed with a replica bat which I had purchased from a local joke shop. Before setting off I put the bat into a specialbox I used for transporting these creatures. The old lady said she had seen the bat in the spare room and I asked her to give me fifteen minutes to search the room. I sat on the bed for that period of time making bumping noises to reassure the lady that I was searching. I then emerged with the bat box saying that she needn't worry anymore because I had found the bat. I opened the box just a fraction and let the lady peep inside. When she saw the bat she was so delighted and I told her that there would not be any more bats.

Two days later I received a phone call from the psychiatrist who was treating the dear old lady. He complimented me on coming up with a solution to the bat problem and said it would be instrumental in working towards a cure for her. I only hope she continued to recover, as the only cost to me was three sleepless nights and a rubber bat.

Someone did remark that it could have been worse; it could have been a crocodile.

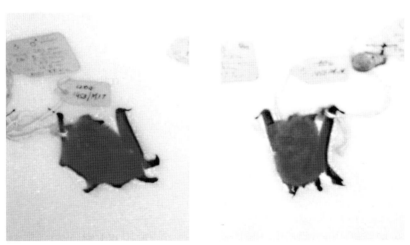

common pipistrelle bats

Badger Rescue

It is very difficult for me to write about some aspects of animal rescues. I suppose we all want to see the good side of life and to shut out the nasties but reality is always around the corner. So many of my rescues have had happy endings, with that great feeling of satisfaction of seeing a wild creature being released into its own environment after many weeks or sometimes months of worry, wondering whether that creature is going to survive.

I remember being called out to a remote countryside area above one of the villages near Scarborough, to a badger which was caught in a snare. The weather was to say the least atrocious; there was a force eight gale blowing from the sea accompanied by hail. I had to park my jeep some three-quarters of a mile from where our badger was reported to be because the terrain was too rough to allow me to drive any closer. This meant for the rest of the way I had to physically carry a large specially built container for animals which don't like to be contained and various cutting tools. The going was very tough indeed as it had been snowing earlier; I was wet, cold and very much fed up with the whole situation. I kept thinking about the person who had subjected the badger to so much suffering and leaving it so that yours truly had to battle with the elements in order to release it. This person was very unpopular indeed. I reached the spot where the badger was trapped, it was an adult male, and at first sighting my heart sank because there was no movement. He was curled up in a ball as if he was too worn out to struggle any further. I could see a circular trench where he had gone round in circles trying to free himself from this cruel piece of equipment. He was not the beautiful black and white badger as we all know, but a pathetic mud covered ball of misery.

As I approached him to cut off the snare I noticed some movement and to my surprise he was actually sleeping. This certainly threw a different light on the subject, this chap was not going to let me cut the wire without a struggle. I was right! He awoke and on seeing me began to growl; after all I was a human, an animal he certainly did not trust. I put on a pair of gloves especially designed for protection against animals which are rather partial to a finger or two, and our badger was no exception. My first move was a psychological approach. I sat on a log some three feet away from my new friend or enemy depending on how you saw the situation. I did not look directly at him because to do so only increases the stress on the animal. I spoke to him in a very soft voice. I don't remember exactly what I said, it was something like, 'Hello little man. How on earth have you got yourself into such a mess?' and, 'Never mind we will soon get you out.' I don't know why I said we, as I was alone on this one. I have always found that if a soft approach is made to animals the task of rescue is made much easier.

Getting back to the rescue in hand, my badger was fairly relaxed so I approached him very slowly with the wire cutters in a heavily gloved hand. The badger was sitting perfectly still at this stage until I was within inches of him. He then made one almighty grab for my hand. Luckily it was the free one. He sank his teeth into the thick metal studded leather and held on tight. He had that look in his eye as if to say, 'Gotcha!' This gave me the chance I was looking for; it enabled me to cut the wire which then slipped from his neck. I slipped my hand out of the glove that he was holding, which in turn he dropped, perhaps he knew there were no tasty fingers inside. For several seconds he sat, perhaps not realizing that he was free. I looked to see if there was any damage to his neck and to my surprise and relief there was none. He then suddenly made off very quickly up a narrow path leading into a rather dense wood. He was free!

The story does not end there because as I stood watching my badger disappearing into the thick undergrowth I heard a disturbance not far away from where I was standing. I went to investigate and I could not believe what I saw. There was another badger in the same difficulties as the one I had just released. There was quite a lot of blood about; the poor soul had not been as lucky and needed rescuing immediately. This meant a quite different and speedier approach than the first one. The only way in which I was going to get this badger into the carrying case was to cut the snare from the tree to which it was fastened and use it as if it were a dog lead. I knew that the badger must not escape because his injuries could be serious.

I proceeded to cut some of the entangled undergrowth between two trees where I intended to put the carrying case. The object was to let the badger think that the open end of the carrying case was his only way of escape. I put the carrying case between the two trees and laid branches on top. After making sure that everything was in place and the badger was facing towards the open mouth of the carrying case I held on tightly to the snare wire and cut it. The badger immediately shot into the carrying case as if he were jet propelled and I, almost as fast, closed the door. I had won! Who cared if I was wet, muddy, cold, tired and wishing that I had chosen to be a pop star rather than a wildlife rescuer. It was a long, difficult trek back to the jeep.

The irony of this incident is that the happy ending, for me, wasn't so happy at all. I lived in a large house in the centre of Scarborough, and when I arrived with the badger I went straight into the room which I used for treating my patients, so that I could cut the snare from around the badger's neck and assess his injuries. I examined the badger thoroughly and I was delighted to find that he wasn't seriously injured so I was able to treat him myself. Someone from the Badger Protection Group was on their way to collect the badger and I had left the front door open for them. Next morning I went to the freezer and discovered it was empty except for two loaves of bread. Someone had slipped in while I was treating the badger, and as Christmas was just around the corner I wasn't the happiest person in the world. I went to collect my jacket; it wasn't there!

I made a few enquiries as to why the snares were there in the first place. I was told on good authority that this type of snare is quite legal. It is designed not to kill, but to restrain the trapped animal, and are used by gamekeepers and farmers to catch foxes. They are advised to check them periodically to ensure that no domestic or protected creatures become caught in the snares. It is just a thought; I wonder what would happen to the poor unfortunate creatures if because of heavy snow conditions the snares could not be visited. I leave you to draw your own conclusions.

It Fell of a Lorry

This story begins about three weeks before Christmas. Things were ticking over quite well and there had been very few rescues to carry out.

I answered a phone call from a very excited lady. She told me she was looking after a turkey which had fallen off the back of a lorry. I thought, someone is pulling my leg. I replied that I was in the business of rescuing wild creatures, not receiving stolen property.

The lady then began to explain in detail what had happened. She was walking on the main Bridlington to Scarborough road; a lorry passed her loaded with turkeys in cages. One of the cages toppled off the lorry and when it hit the road out popped a very frightened bird. She only lived a short distance from where the turkey had landed and she managed to coax him into her garden. She gave the turkey some bread and rice and while he was feeding she rang me.

I arrived at the lady's house and sure enough there was a very happy turkey, and why not? He certainly wasn't going onto someone's plate on Christmas Day. I thanked the lady on both my own and the turkey's behalf and assured her that I would keep her informed of his progress. I decided to call the turkey Lucky. Not very original, as many rescued creatures are christened the same. I did, however, feel that this bird would most certainly have died on arrival at his destination. When I arrived home I made Lucky comfortable and gave him a large dish of barley. I thought he was unusually friendly, or perhaps I thought so because I was accustomed to frightened wild birds and not domestic fowl. My next task was to contact the local newspaper to put an ad in the lost and found column. I hoped I wouldn't receive any replies.

The editor saw the ad and rang me. I told him the story and he immediately wanted to print a feature and photo for Christmas. A few days after the story had been printed the phone never stopped ringing. The national press had got hold of the story. A reporter arrived with a photographer who brought a small Christmas tree and some tinsel. He photographed Lucky standing in front of the tree with the tinsel around his neck. Soon after the story went into the national press I received a phone call from a researcher from BBC Radio 5. She asked me if I would be willing to do a Christmas Day interview. The interview was to draw the public's attention to the people throughout the UK who worked on Christmas Day. I agreed. The broadcast was to take place several miles from Scarborough in an outside broadcast unit at a racing stable. This meant I had to get up at 4.am on Christmas Day, feed all my patients and arrive at 7.am. The interview was scheduled to go out at 7.30a.m. When I arrived I was introduced to the interviewer who led me to a very large mobile studio. Inside there seemed to be dials, switches and people everywhere. I can only describe it as something like the Starship Enterprise. I heard voices which they said were coming from London. Surely they didn't think that I thought they were coming from outer space? The interviewer briefed me on what she was going to ask me when we were on the air. I assured her that everything would be all right as I had become accustomed to media interviews and I never got stuck for words. She also said she would have preferred some live turkey noises. I suggested that the interview went ahead as scheduled and I would make the turkey noises. The interviewer was delighted. Her staff and engineers chuckled. At precisely 7.30am the interview began and I was introduced to the nation. Everything went smoothly until the interviewer pretended to ask Lucky a question and point-

ed to me. I looked at the engineers and assistants who were trying not to laugh; there was a brief silence which to me felt like hours, then out it came, 'Gobble, gobble.' The interviewer concluded the interview, gave a sigh of relief and like everyone else burst into riotous laughter.

Over the next few days people asked me how I got the turkey to say 'gobble gobble' at that particular moment? I never let them into the secret. Lucky was eventually adopted by a country family. They gave me their word that he would remain with them as a family pet for the rest of his natural life.

Good Companions

You may have noticed that I have only mentioned four domestic animals in this book, my childhood pet dog, Trixie, and Max the Alsatian, the Rottweiler and the puppy rescued from the River Aire. That doesn't imply that I was not involved with domestic animals, on the contrary, I operated a financial scheme to help people on low income with their vets' bills. I also operated a free neutering and spaying service for dogs, which was my contribution to help reduce the huge problem of unwanted puppies. Unfortunately, I was reluctantly forced to cease these services due to lack of funds. Needless to say there were times when a pet needed rescuing.

A young man came into my shop one Saturday morning and told me that his dog, a terrier named Tweed, had chased after something down a rabbit burrow and hadn't returned home. He said that Tweed had done this before and managed to get out, but not this time. He had tried to dig Tweed out without success. I said to him, 'Don't worry; I will soon get Tweed out.' I asked him, 'When did Tweed go down the hole?' He replied, 'Last Wednesday. That's why I have called in to ask for your help.'

We arrived at the spot where the dog had disappeared. It was a very steep embankment made up of sandy soil. I felt that there could be very little hope of finding the poor unfortunate creature alive. I asked the young man to call the dog's name, which he did; there was a faint whimper from deep down inside the rabbit warren. I started to dig in the direction of where I thought the sound was coming from, but unfortunately the sandy soil kept falling in and blocking the entrance to the burrow. It was like driving in thick fog. I found a long stick which I used as a probe. This enabled me to keep track of which direction the burrow was going. I was digging for about an hour without much success. We could still hear the weak whimpering but it seemed much further away as time went by. I was becoming quite tired, so I decided to get our local fire brigade to assist as I knew they would be better equipped than me for such a rescue. They arrived, followed by a local newspaper reporter and photographer. After nearly two hours of digging and listening, and following the many yards of burrows which veered in so many directions, we were still no closer to a rescue. I suggested that we push a rod into the soil in order to find a burrow and then dig straight down, as I had when I began the rescue attempt, thus saving time and effort. My fellow diggers agreed and after about half an hour the whimpering got closer. To the delight of everyone the little dog finally appeared. I pulled him out to the cheers of all involved and I think I detected a tear in the eyes of our fire crew who had toiled endlessly for over three hours. Tweed looked quite thin and a little unkempt so the young man promptly took him home for a meal and a bath.

Several years have passed since that incident and just recently when I was sitting enjoying a cup of tea at my favourite cafe a man approached me and said, 'Do you remember me?' 'Sorry, no, I don't,' I replied. 'You rescued my dog from a rabbit hole a few years ago and I just want to say thank you.'

Nostalgic Return

I will finish this book where it began so to speak, in the village of Newlay.

I recently visited the village, some fifty years on. The old bridge is still there, looking very impressive having being extensively renovated in 1983/84.

Of course the river, now much cleaner, and the weir are still there, but alas, the most important things in a schoolboy's life and in a sixty-seven-year-old's are gone forever. Nearly all of the beautiful woodland which I considered mine has made way for a housing estate.

I sat and pondered on the river bank. I wondered if the grandchildren of many generations of Boris, my friendly water vole, were still on the river bank or if they had also disappeared like so many beautiful things I remembered.

I hoped I would find close by a special old sycamore tree. I searched for a little while feeling all kinds of emotions. Surprisingly it did not take long to find the tree and I thought it was wearing much better than me. I looked at the initials carved on the trunk: DK, BC, TP, GA and of course JW, 1942, the initials of my school pals and myself. I wonder where they are today?

I was happy to return, though I did shed a tear or two and wished I could turn the clock back.

*I hope you have enjoyed reading my book
as much as I enjoyed writing it.*

I pray there will be many more little Jim Wards with that

'Wild Understanding'.